MISSIONARY HEROES IN ASIA

Dr. Chamberlain was quite unaware that a Huge Serpent was hanging over him

MISSIONARY HEROES IN ASIA

TRUE STORIES OF THE INTREPID BRAVERY AND STIRRING ADVENTURES OF MISSONARIES WITH UNCIVILIZED MAN, WILD BEASTS AND THE FORCES OF NATURE

BY

JOHN C. LAMBERT, M.A., D.D.

AUTHOR OF
"THE OMNIPOTENT CROSS," "THREE FISHING BOATS"

WITH TEN ILLUSTRATIONS

GYAN

Published by

Gyan Publishing House
5, Ansari Road
Daryaganj, New Delhi-110002
Phone: 011-47034999, 9811692060
E-mail: books@gyanbooks.com

Distribution Network
gyanbooks.com
India, USA, Canada, UK, Australia, France

ISBN : 978-81-212-3783-3 (PB)
First Published, 1908

2nd Impression 2020

Printed at: Gyan Press, Delhi.

Missionary Heroes in Asia
Author: John C. Lambert

UNIFORM WITH THIS VOLUME

THE PINK LIBRARY

BOOKS FOR BOYS & GIRLS

With many Illustrations. Extra Crown 8vo.

By the Rev. Canon E. C. DAWSON.

LION-HEARTED. The Story of Bishop Hannington's Life Told for Boys and Girls.

By M. L. CHARLESWORTH.

THE OLD LOOKING-GLASS AND THE BROKEN LOOKING-GLASS. In One Volume.

By the Rev. A. J. CHURCH.

TO THE LIONS. A Tale of the Early Christians.
A GREEK GULLIVER.

By Bishop WILBERFORCE.

AGATHOS. The Rocky Island, and other Sunday Stories.

By Mrs. CAREY BROCK.

DAME WYNTON'S HOME. A Tale Illustrative of the Lord's Prayer.

By EMMA MARSHALL.

BROTHERS AND SISTERS.
BROOK SILVERTONE.

By E. BERTHET.

THE WILD MAN OF THE WOODS.

By MARY SEELEY.

THE WORLD BEFORE THE FLOOD. Stories from the Best Book.

By the Rev. J. C. LAMBERT, M.A., D.D.

MISSIONARY HEROES IN ASIA.

By L. M. ALCOTT.

LITTLE WOMEN.

By VARIOUS AUTHORS.

THE LIFE OF A BEAR. With Sixteen Illustrations.
THE LIFE OF AN ELEPHANT. With Sixteen Illustrations.
ONLY A DOG. By a Humble Friend. With Eight Illustrations.

SEELEY & CO., LIMITED

PREFATORY NOTE

THE author desires with much gratitude to acknowledge his debt to the following ladies and gentlemen, who have most kindly assisted him in gathering the materials for this book by giving their consent to his use of their writings, by lending him books and photographs, or in other ways :—

The Rev. George Robson, D.D., Editor of the "Missionary Record of the United Free Church of Scotland"; the Rev. E. P. Cachemaille, M.A., and Captain E. Poulden, R.N.; the Rev. J. W. Jack, M.A.; the Rev. W. MacNaughtan, M.A.; Miss M. G. Cowan, Hon. Librarian of the Missionary Library at Lady Stair's House, Edinburgh; Mr. John Cochrane, of the Publications Office of the United Free Church.

He would also express his obligations to the following missionary societies and firms of publishers, which have most courteously allowed him to make use of the books mentioned in their proper places at the end of each chapter, and in some cases of illustrations of which they hold the copyright :—

The South American Society ; the Religious Tract Society ; The Clarendon Press ; Messrs. Oliphant, Anderson, & Ferrier ; The Fleming H. Revell Co. ; Messrs. Hodder & Stoughton ; Messrs. Morgan & Scott.

INTRODUCTION

IN a "foreword" which he contributes to Dr. Jacob Chamberlain's attractive missionary book, *In the Tiger Jungle*, Dr. Francis E. Clark expresses the opinion that one need not patronize sensational and unhealthy fiction to find stirring adventure and thrilling narrative, and then goes on to say:—

"There is one source which furnishes stories of intense and dramatic interest, abounding in novel situations and spiced with abundant adventure; and this source is at the same time the purest and most invigorating fountain at which our youth can drink. To change the figure, this is a mine hitherto largely unworked; it contains rich nuggets of ore, which will well repay the prospector in this new field."

The field to which Dr. Clark refers is the history of modern Christian missions. His meaning is that the adventurous and stirring side of missionary experience needs to be brought out, and emphasis laid upon the fact that the romantic days of missions are by no means past.

There are stories which are now among the classics of missionary romance. Such are the expedition of Hans Egede to Greenland, the lonely journeys of David Brainerd among the Indian tribes of the North American forests, the voyage of John Williams from one coral island of the Pacific to another in the little ship which his own hands had built, the exploration of the Dark Continent by David Livingstone in the hope of emancipating the black man's soul.

But among missionary lives which are more recent or less known, there are many not less noble or less thrilling than those just referred to; and the chapters which follow are an attempt to make this plain.

There is, of course, a deeper side to Christian missions—a side that is essential and invariable—while the elements of adventure and romance are accidental and occasional. If in these pages the spiritual aspects of foreign mission work are but slightly touched upon, it is not because they are either forgotten or ignored, but simply because it was not part of the writer's present plan to deal with them. It is hoped, nevertheless, that some of those into whose hands this book may come will be induced by what they read to make fuller acquaintance with the lives and aims of our missionary heroes, and so will catch something of that spirit which led them to face innumerable dangers, toils, and trials among heathen and often savage peoples, whether in the frozen North or the burning South, whether in the hidden depths of some vast continent or among the scattered "islands of the ocean seas."

In the recently published *Memoirs of Archbishop Temple* we find the future Primate of the Church of England, when a youth of twenty, writing to tell his mother how his imagination had been stirred by the sight of Bishop Selwyn of New Zealand starting for the Pacific with a band of young men who had devoted themselves to the propagation of the Gospel among a benighted and barbarous people. "It is not mere momentary enthusiasm with me," he writes; "my heart beats whenever I think of it. I think it one of the noblest things England has done for a long time; almost the only thing really worthy of herself."

It is the author's earnest desire that the narratives which follow may help to kindle in some minds an enthusiasm for missions like that which characterized Frederick Temple to the very end of his long and strenuous life; or, better still, that they may even suggest to some who are looking forward to the future with a high ambition, and wondering how to make the most of life, whether there is any career which offers so many opportunities of romantic experience and heroic achievement as that of a Christian missionary.

CONTENTS

Contents

CHAPTER IV

"FROM FAR FORMOSA"

CHAPTER V

A HEROINE OF TIBET

CHAPTER VI

"THE SAVIOUR OF LIAO-YANG"

LIST OF ILLUSTRATIONS

PUBLISHERS' NOTE

THE contents of this volume have been taken from Dr. Lambert's larger book, entitled "The Romance of Missionary Heroism," published at five shillings.

IN THE STEPPES AND DESERTS OF MONGOLIA

Missionary Heroes in Asia

CHAPTER I

IN THE STEPPES AND DESERTS OF MONGOLIA

James Gilmour—His bold plan—Mongolia—Across the plains—Boarding in a lama's tent—A Mongol menu—Scotch porridge—Learning to ride—Gilmour as pedlar and tramp—Wolves and bandits—The man in the iron cage—The wounded soldier and the living skeleton—Robinson Crusoe turned missionary.

ABOUT the middle of the year 1870 there arrived in Peking a young Scotchman, James Gilmour by name, who had been sent out to China by the London Missionary Society to begin work in the capital. Within a few weeks of his arrival, there took place at Tientsin, the port of Peking, that fanatical outbreak known as the Tientsin massacre, in which a Roman Catholic convent was destroyed and thirteen French people murdered. A widespread panic at once took hold of the capital. The European community felt that they were living on the edge of a volcano, for no one knew but that this massacre might be the prelude to a general outburst of anti-foreign hatred such as was witnessed later in connexion with the Boxer movement. All around Gilmour his acquaintances were packing up their most precious belongings, and holding themselves in readiness for a hurried flight to the south. It was at this moment that the new-comer resolved on a bold and original move. Instead of fleeing to the south in search of safety, he would turn his face northwards and see if no opening could be found for Christian work among the Mongols of the great Mongolian plains. He was utterly unacquainted both with the country and the language, but he had long felt a deep and romantic interest in that vast, lonely plateau which lies between China proper and Siberia, and forms by far the largest dependency of the Chinese Empire. The suspension of work in Peking seemed to offer the very opportunity he wanted for pushing his way into Mongolia. And so as soon as the necessary preparations could be made, for Gilmour was never the man to let the grass grow beneath his feet, he left the capital behind with all its rumours and alarms. Before long the Great Wall was passed, which ever since the third century B.C. has defended China from Mongolia. And then, with two camels and a camel-cart, our intrepid traveller set his face towards the Desert of Gobi, which lies in the very heart of the Mongolian plain.

Mongolia, the home of the Mongols, has been described as a rough parallelogram, 1800 miles from east to west, and 1000 miles from north to south. It is a huge plateau lifted high above the sea, in part desert, in part a treeless expanse of grassy steppe, and in part covered by mountain ranges whose peaks rise up to the line of perpetual snow. The climate, hot and dry in summer and bitterly cold in winter, makes agriculture impossible except in some favoured spots, and so by the force of his circumstances the Mongol is a nomad, dwelling in a tent, and pasturing his flocks and herds upon the grass of the steppe. For long centuries the people were a constant terror to the Chinese. Even the Great Wall proved an ineffectual barrier against them, and time and again they poured like a mighty flood over the rich lands of their peace-loving neighbours to the south. But about 500 years ago they were converted from their earlier Pagan faith to Buddhism in its corrupted form of Lamaism, and this change of faith has had a decidedly softening effect upon the national character. Much of this, no doubt, must be attributed to the custom which prevails among them of devoting one or more sons in every family to the priesthood. One result of this custom is, that the Mongol priests, or lamas as they are called, actually form the majority of the male population, and as the lamas are celibates in virtue of their office, another result has been a great reduction in the population, as compared with early days. It is calculated that at the present time there are not more than two millions of Mongols occupying this vast territory of 1,300,000 square miles. Mongolia is no longer entitled now to the name it once received of *officina gentium,* "the manufactory of nations." It does not now possess those surplus swarms of bold and warlike horsemen which it once sent out to overrun and conquer other lands. But, like all nomads, its people are still an active and hardy race. As horsemen, too, they still excel. From their very infancy both men and women are accustomed to the saddle, and even yet some of them could rival the feats of the horsemen of Ghengis Khan, the greatest of all the Mongol conquerors of long ago. It was to this country and this interesting, but little known, people that James Gilmour devoted his life.

His first journey across the great plateau began at Kalgan, which lies to the north-west of Peking, just within the Great Wall, and terminated at Kiachta on the southern frontier of Siberia. He made his journey over plain and desert, which occupied only a month, in the company of a Russian official who knew no English, while he himself knew neither Russian nor Mongolian. He was glad, therefore, on reaching Kiachta to meet a fellow-countryman, one of the world's ubiquitous

Scots, in the person of a trader named Grant. Grant was exceedingly kind to him, and took him into his own comfortable house. But finding that this contact with civilization was hindering him in his strenuous efforts to master the Mongolian language without delay, Gilmour formed a characteristic resolution. This was nothing else than to go out upon the plain and try to persuade some Mongolian to receive him as an inmate of his tent.

It was at night that this idea occurred to him, and the next morning he left Kiachta, taking nothing with him but his "Penang lawyer." This, it should be explained, is a heavy walking-stick, so called because in Penang it is supposed to be useful in settling disputes. Gilmour had already discovered that in Mongolia it was not only useful, but altogether indispensable, as a protection against the ferocious assaults of the wolfish-looking dogs which invariably rush at a traveller if he draws near to any encampment. One of the first incidents of the caravan journey from Kalgan had been the narrow escape of a Russian soldier from being torn down by a

In a Mongol Encampment

Mr. Gilmour always dressed in Chinese clothes, and when on tour generally had a postman's bag strapped over one shoulder and a waterproof fishing-bag over the other, these two containing all his baggage.

pack of Mongolian dogs. With a stout "limb of the law" in his fist, however, Gilmour feared nothing, but strode cheerfully over the plain, making for the first tent he saw on the horizon.

As he drew near he heard the sound of a monotonous voice engaged in some kind of chant, and when he entered found a lama at his prayers. The lama, hearing footsteps, looked round and pronounced the one word, "Sit!" and then continued his devotions. For another quarter of an hour he went on, taking no further notice of his visitor meanwhile. But suddenly his droning chant ceased, and he came forward and gave Gilmour a hospitable welcome. Gilmour opened his mind to him without delay, telling him that it was his desire to spend the winter in his tent and learn Mongolian from his instruction. The lama was surprised, but perfectly willing, and agreed to receive his visitor as a paying guest for an indefinite period at the modest rate of about a shilling a day. And so within a few months of his departure from London we find Gilmour living the life of a nomad in the tent of a lama on the Mongolian plain.

Once the first novelty had worn off, he found the life somewhat monotonous. Dinner was the great event of the day, the more so as it is the only meal in which a Mongol indulges. The preparations for this repast were unvarying, as also was the subsequent menu. Towards sunset the lama's servant, who was himself a lama, melted a block of ice in a huge pot, over a fire which filled the tent with smoke. Taking a hatchet, he next hewed a solid lump of mutton from a frozen carcase and put it into the water. As soon as it was boiled, he fished it out with the fire-tongs and laid it on a board before his master and Gilmour, who then attacked it with fingers and knives. Forks were things unknown. When a Mongol eats he takes a piece of meat in his left hand, seizes it with his teeth, and then cuts off his mouthful close to his lips by a quick upward movement of his knife. The operation looks dangerous, but the flatness of the native nose makes it safe enough, though it would be very risky in the case of one who was otherwise endowed. The Mongols always thought Gilmour's nose tremendous, and they excused him for cutting off his mouthfuls first and appropriating them afterwards.

Meanwhile, as this first course was in progress, the servant had thrown some millet into the water used for boiling the meat, and when the diners had partaken sufficiently of the fare, this thin gruel was served up as a kind of soup. The mutton, Gilmour says, was tough; but he declares that seldom in his life did he taste any preparation of civilized cookery so delicious as this millet-soup. He admits that he has no doubt that it was chiefly desert-hunger that made it seem so good.

Though he ate only once a day, the lama, like all Mongols, consumed vast quantities of tea. At dawn, and again at noon, the servant prepared a pailful of the cheering beverage, giving it always ten or fifteen minutes' hard boiling, and seasoning it with fat and a little meal instead of milk. Gilmour accommodated himself to the ways of the tent. As a concession to his Scotch tastes, however, he was provided every morning with a cupful of meal made into something like porridge by the addition of boiling water. This the lama and his servant called

"Scotland," and they were careful to set it aside regularly for the use of "Our Gilmour," to whom, Buddhist priests though they were, they soon became quite attached.

Before leaving the subject of meals, we may mention that on the last day of the year Mongols make up for their abstemiousness during the other 364 by taking no fewer than seven dinners. When New Year's Eve arrived, the lama insisted that his visitor should do his duty like a Mongolian, and a yellow-coated old lama, who was present as a guest on the occasion, was told off to keep count of his progress. Gilmour managed to put down three dinners, and was just wondering what to do next when he discovered that his guardian lama had got drunk and lost count. In this case, although himself a strict teetotaller, he did not feel disposed to take too severe a view of the old gentleman's failing.

When the time came at last to recross the plains, Gilmour decided to make the homeward journey on horseback instead of by camel-cart. The one drawback was that he had never yet learned to ride. But as he had found that the best way to learn Mongolian was by being compelled to speak it, he considered that a ride of a good many hundred miles might be the best way of learning to sit on a horse. The plan proved a decided success. In Mongolia a man who cannot ride is looked upon as a curiosity, and when Gilmour first mounted everybody turned out to enjoy the sight of his awkwardness. But though he had one or two nasty falls through his horse stumbling into holes on treacherous bits of ground, such as are very frequent on the plains, where the rats have excavated galleries underground, he soon learned to be quite at home on the back of his steed. When he rode at last once more through a gateway of the Great Wall, passing thus out of Mongolia into China again, he felt that after the training he had received on his way across the steppes and the desert, he would be ready henceforth to take to the saddle in any circumstances. Indeed, so sure of his seat had he become that we find him on a subsequent occasion, when he formed one of a company mounted for a journey on Chinese mules, which will not travel except in single file, riding with his face to the tail of his beast, so as to be better able to engage in conversation with the cavalier who came behind him.

This crossing and recrossing of the Mongolian plain, and especially the winter he had spent in the lama's tent, had already given Gilmour a knowledge of the Mongolian language, and a familiarity with the habits and thoughts of the Mongols themselves, such as hardly any other Western could pretend to. Peking, when he returned to it, had settled down to something like its normal quiet, but he felt that the ordinary routine of work in the city was not the work to which he was specially called. The desert air was in his blood now, and Mongolia was calling. Henceforth it was for the Mongols that he lived.

Year by year Gilmour fared forth into the Great Plain in prosecution of his chosen task. And although it was his custom to return to Peking for the winter, he still continued while there to devote himself to his Mongol flock. Between China and Mongolia a considerable trade is carried on, the Mongols bringing in hides, cheese, butter, and the other products of a pastoral territory, and carrying away in return vast quantities of cheap tea in the form of compressed bricks, these bricks being used in Gilmour's time not only for the preparation of the favourite beverage, but as a means of exchange in lieu of money. During the winter months large numbers of traders arrive in Peking from all parts of Mongolia, and many of them camp out in their tents in open spaces, just as they do when living on the plains. Gilmour frequented these encampments, and took every opportunity he could make or find of conversing about religious matters, and especially of seeking to commend "the Jesus-doctrine," as the Buddhists called it. One plan that he followed was to go about like a Chinese pedlar, with two bags of books in the Mongolian language hanging from his shoulders. All were invited to buy, and in many cases this literature was taken up quite eagerly. Often a would-be purchaser demanded to have a book read aloud to him before he made up his mind about it, and this gave the pedlar a welcome chance of reading from the Gospels to the crowd which gathered, and then of introducing a conversation, which sometimes passed into a discussion, about the merits of Jesus and Buddha. Sometimes those who were anxious to buy had no money, but were prepared to pay in kind. And so, not infrequently, Gilmour was to be seen at night making his way back to his lodgings in the city "with a miscellaneous collection of cheese, sour-curd, butter, millet-cake, and sheep's fat, representing the produce of part of the day's sales."

Among the most remarkable of Gilmour's many journeys through Mongolia was one which he made in 1884, and made entirely on foot. He was a tremendous walker at times, more perhaps by reason of his unusual will power than because of exceptional physical strength, and is known to have covered 300 miles in seven and a half days—an average of forty miles a day. On the occasion of his long tramp over the plains and back, he had special reasons for adopting that method of locomotion.

One was that grass was so scarce during that year that it would hardly have been possible to get pasture for a camel or a horse.

Another was that the love of simplicity and unconventionality, which was so marked a feature of his character, grew stronger and stronger, and also the desire to get as near as possible to the poorest and humblest of the people. At a later period we find him adopting in its entirety "not only the native dress, but practically the native food, and so far as a Christian man could, native habits of life." An idea of the length to which he carried the rule of plain living may be gathered from the fact that for some time his rate of expenditure was only threepence a day. His biographer, Mr. Lovett, gives us a graphic picture of him taking his bowl of porridge, native fashion, in the street, sitting down upon a low stool beside the boiler of the itinerant vendor from whom he had just purchased it. And the plainness of his garb at times may be judged of when we mention that in one village on the borders of China he was turned out of the two respectable inns which the place could boast, on the ground that he was a foot-traveller without cart or animal, who must be content to betake himself to the tavern for tramps.

It was in keeping with his tastes, therefore, as well as from necessity, that he once tramped through Mongolia with all his belongings on his back. His equipment when he set out consisted of a postman's brown bag on one side, containing his kit and provisions; on the other an angler's waterproof bag with books, etc.; together with a Chinaman's sheepskin coat slung over his shoulder by means of a rough stick of the "Penang lawyer" type. In the course of this tramp, his formidable stick notwithstanding, he had sometimes to be rescued from the teeth of the dogs which flew, not unnaturally, at a character so suspicious-looking. But he met with much hospitality from the people, both lamas and laymen, wherever he went; and returned to Kalgan without any serious mishap. From two dangers of the country he altogether escaped. One was the risk of being attacked by wolves, which are a perfect terror to the Chinese traveller over the plains, though the inhabitants themselves make light of them, and never hesitate when they catch sight of one to become the attacking party. The result of this is that a wolf is said to distinguish from afar between a Mongol and a Chinaman, slinking off as hastily as possible if it sees a wayfarer approaching in long skin robes, but anticipating a good dinner at the sight of another in blue jacket and trousers. Gilmour himself was of opinion that Mongolian wolves are not so dangerous as Siberian ones. The reason he gives is that, unlike the Russians, the Mongols keep such poor sheep-folds that a wolf can help itself to a sheep whenever it likes, and so is seldom driven by hunger to attack a man. The other danger was from bandits. For there are parts of the Desert of Gobi, crossed as it is by the great trade routes between Siberia and China, which are quite as unpleasant to traverse as the ancient road between Jerusalem and Jericho. But Gilmour was probably never more secure against highway robbery than when he walked through Mongolia as a missionary tramp.

It is impossible to enter into the details of the strange and romantic experiences which befell this adventurous spirit in the course of his many wanderings. Now we find him spending the night in a lama's tent, most probably discussing sacred things with his host till far on towards morning over a glowing fire of *argol*, or dried cow's dung, the customary fuel of the plains. At another time he is careering across the desert on horseback as swiftly as his Mongol companions, for he was a man who never liked to be beaten. Now he is at a marriage feast, looking on with observant and humorous eyes at the rough but harmless merry-makings. Again, he is in a court of justice, where punishment is meted out on the spot upon the culprit's back, in the presence of a highly appreciative crowd. At one time, with a heart full of pity for a superstitious and deluded people, he is watching a Buddhist turning his praying-wheel with his own hand or hanging it up in front of his tent to be turned for him by the wind. At another, as he passes a criminal in an iron cage who is condemned to be starved to death, and is set day by day in front of an eating-house in a large trading settlement for the aggravation of his tortures, he is reflecting on the defects of a religion that can permit its followers to enjoy this public exhibition of a fellow-creature's dying pains. In his journeys he was constantly exposed to the bitter cold of a land where the thermometer falls in winter to thirty or forty degrees below zero, and all through the heat of summer huge lumps of ice remain unmelted in the wells. Often he had to endure long spells of hunger and thirst when on the march. Worst of all, he had to share the filth and vermin of a Mongol tent as well as its hospitality. But these things he looked upon as all "in the day's work"; and though he may sometimes chronicle them in his diary as facts, he never makes them matter of complaint.

Among the most interesting incidents which he records are some in connexion with his endeavours to bring relief to those whom he found in sickness and pain. Although not a doctor by profession, he had picked up some medical and surgical skill, and did not hesitate to use it on behalf of those for whom no better skill was available. In doing this he sometimes ran great risks, for with all their hospitality the Mongols are terribly suspicious, and ready to entertain the most extraordinary rumours about the designs of any stranger.

Once he persuaded a blind man to come with him to Peking, to have his eyes operated on for cataract in the hospital there. The operation was unsuccessful, and the story was spread over a large region that Gilmour enticed people to Peking in order to steal "the jewels of their eyes" that he might preserve them in a bottle and sell them for hundreds of taels. In consequence of this he lived for months under what almost amounted to sentence of death. Only by showing no consciousness of fear and by patiently living suspicion down, did he escape from being murdered.

Once he had undertaken to treat a soldier for a bullet wound received in an encounter with brigands, thinking that it was only a flesh wound he had to deal with. It turned out to be a difficult bone complication. Now Gilmour knew hardly anything of anatomy, and he had absolutely no books to consult. "What could I do," he says, "but pray?" And a strange thing happened. There tottered up to him through the crowd a live skeleton—a man whose bones literally stood out as distinctly as if he were a specimen in an anatomical museum, with only a yellow skin drawn loosely over them. The man came to beg for cough medicine, but Gilmour was soon busy fingering a particular part of his skeleton, with so strange a smile on his face that he heard a bystander remark, "That smile means something." "So it did," Gilmour adds. "It meant among other things that I knew what to do with the wounded soldier's damaged bone; and in a short time his wound was in a fair way of healing."

James Gilmour's *Among the Mongols* is a book to be read, not only for the romance of its subject-matter, but because of the author's remarkable gift of realistic statement—his power of making his readers see things in bodily presence just as his own eyes had seen them. In more ways than one he reminds us of Borrow, but especially in what Borrow himself described as "the art of telling a plain story." On the first appearance of *Among the Mongols* a very competent reviewer in the *Spectator* traced a striking resemblance in Gilmour to a still greater writer of English than the author of *Lavengro* and *The Bible in Spain.* "Robinson Crusoe," he said, "has turned missionary, lived years in Mongolia, and written a book about it. That is this book." It was high praise, but it contained no small degree of truth. And to the advantage of Gilmour's book as compared with Defoe's, it must be remembered that everything that the former tells us is literally true.

AUTHORITIES.—*Among the Mongols*, by the Rev. James Gilmour, M.A., and *James Gilmour of Mongolia*, by Richard Lovett, M.A. (Religious Tract Society); *The Far East*, by Archibald Little (The Clarendon Press).

IN THE COUNTRY OF THE TELUGUS

CHAPTER II

IN THE COUNTRY OF THE TELUGUS

Indian race-groups—The Dravidians—The land of the Telugus—Dr. Jacob Chamberlain—A primitive ambulance—"The Divine Guru"—Under the "Council-tree"—the village Swami—A Mohammedan mob—Fight with a serpent—The "serpent destroyer" and the village elders—Some tiger adventures—A flood on the Godavery.

APART from the Tibeto-Burman tribes scattered along the skirts of the Himalayas, the peoples of India are commonly divided by ethnologists into three great race-groups—the aborigines (often called the Kolarians), the Dravidians, and the Aryans. The aborigines are now found chiefly in the jungles and mountains of the Central Provinces, into which they were driven at a very early period by the Dravidians, the first invaders of India. Mr. Kipling, who has done so much to make India more intelligible to the English, has not forgotten to give us pictures of the aboriginal peoples. Those who are familiar with his fascinating *Jungle Books* will remember the story of "The King's Ankus," and the weird figure of the little Gond hunter who shot the villager with his feathered arrow for the sake of the jewelled ankus, and afterwards was found by Mowgli and Bagheera lying in the forest beaten to death with bamboo rods by a band of thieves who lusted after the same fatal prize.

In "The Tomb of his Ancestors," again, we have a vivid sketch of the mountain Bhils, whose combination of superstition, courage, and loyalty reminds us of the Scottish Highlanders in the days of Prince Charlie. These aborigines of the hills were long neglected by the Church, but much is now being done on their behalf. Dr. Shepherd, for example, a Scotch medical missionary, has carried both the Gospel and the healing powers of modern science into the wild country of the Bhils of Rajputana, and can tell tales of his experiences among them as striking and thrilling as any that have come from the pen of Rudyard Kipling.

The Dravidians, who first overran India and drove the earlier inhabitants into the hills, were afterwards themselves supplanted to a large extent by the more powerful Aryans. These Aryans were members of that same original stock to which the nations of Europe trace their origin, for while one section of the race moved southwards upon India through the Himalayas from the great plains of Central Asia, another flowed to the west and took possession of Europe. By the Aryan invasion of India the Dravidians were pushed for the most part into the southern portion of the vast peninsula, where they have formed ever since a numerous and powerful group. Five Dravidian peoples are usually distinguished, the Tamils and the Telugus being the most important of the five. It is of work among the Telugus that we are to speak in the present chapter.

The country of the Telugus stretches northwards from Madras for some five hundred miles along the shores of the Bay of Bengal, while to the west it extends about half-way across the peninsula, and so includes large parts not only of the Presidency of Madras, but of the kingdom of Mysore and the dominions of the Nizam of Hyderabad. It is a region which attracts those who go to India for sport and adventure, for its jungles still abound in tigers and other wild animals. From the point of view of Christian missions it has this special interest, that there is no part of all Hindustan where the Gospel has been preached with more marked success, or where the people have been gathered more rapidly into the Christian Church.

One of the most enterprising of modern Indian missionaries is Dr. Jacob Chamberlain, of the American Reformed Church, who began his labours as a medical evangelist to the Telugus more than forty years ago. He is the author of two books, *The Cobra's Den* and *In the Tiger Jungle*, which give graphic sketches of his experiences in city and village and jungle, on horseback and in bullock-cart, in the surgery with operating knife in hand, and at the busy fair when a crowd has gathered round and the knife that cures the body has been exchanged for the Book that saves the soul. Taking these two delightful volumes as our authorities, we shall first glance at Dr. Chamberlain in the midst of his medical and surgical work, and see how effective such work becomes in opening the way for Christian teaching. Then we shall follow him on one of his longer evangelistic tours through the Telugu country.

All morning, ever since sunrise, the doctor has been busy with the patients who have come from far and near to be treated or prescribed for, until about a hundred persons are gathered in front of the little dispensary. The heat of the day is now coming on, but before dismissing them and distributing the medicines they have waited for, he takes down his Telugu Bible, reads and explains a chapter, and then kneels to ask a blessing upon all who have need of healing.

It is now breakfast-time, and after several hours of hard work the doctor is quite ready for a good meal. But just as he is about to go home for the purpose, he hears the familiar chant used by the natives when carrying a heavy burden, and looking out sees four men approaching, two in front and two behind, with a long bamboo pole on their shoulders, and a blanket slung on it in hammock fashion with a sick man inside. Behind this primitive ambulance two men are walking, one leading the other by the hand.

In a few minutes the sick man is laid in his blanket on the floor of the verandah, and the little company have told their tale. They have come from a village two days' journey off. They have heard of the foreign doctor that he can work wonderful cures. The young man in the blanket is dying; the old man led by the hand is his uncle, who has recently grown blind. Their friends have brought them to the Doctor Padre to see if he can make them well.

On examination Dr. Chamberlain finds that the young man's case is almost hopeless, but that there is just a chance of saving him by a serious surgical operation—and this he performs the same afternoon. At first the patient seems to be sinking under the shock, but he rallies by and by, and gradually comes back to health and strength again. The old man's blindness is a simpler case. An easy operation and careful treatment are all that are required. And so when uncle and nephew have been in the hospital for a few weeks, the doctor is able to send them back to their village—the young man walking on his own feet, and the old man no longer needing to be led by the hand.

But here the story does not end. Every day while in hospital the two patients had heard the doctor read a chapter from the Gospel and make its meaning plain. And when the time for leaving came they begged for a copy of the history of Yesu Kristu, "the Divine Guru," so that they might let all their neighbours know of the glad news they had heard. They acknowledged that they could not read, for they were poor weavers who had never been to school. "But when the cloth merchant comes to buy our webs," they said, "we will gather the villagers, and put the book into his hand, and say, 'Read us this book, and then we will talk business.' And when the tax-gatherer comes we will say, 'Read us this book, and then we will settle our taxes.' Let us have the book therefore, for we want all our village to know about the Divine Guru, Yesu Kristu."

They got the book and went away, and for three years Dr. Chamberlain heard nothing of them. But at last on a wide preaching tour he met them again. They had learned of his approach, and when he entered the village at sunrise the whole population was gathered under the "Council-tree," while his two patients of three years ago came forward with smiling faces to greet him, and told him that through the reading of the Gospel every one in the place had agreed to give up his idols if the Doctor Padre would send some one to teach them more about Jesus. Dr. Chamberlain discussed the matter fully with them, and when he saw that they were thoroughly in earnest, promised to send a teacher as soon as possible. But just before leaving to proceed on his journey he noticed, near at hand, the little village temple, with its stone idols standing on their platform at the farther end of the shrine.

"What are you going to do with these idols now?" he said to the people.

"The idols are nothing to us any longer," they replied; "we have renounced them all."

"But are you going to leave them standing there in the very heart of the village?"

"What would you have us do with them?" they asked.

"Well," said the doctor, wishing to test their sincerity, "I would like to take one of them away with me." He knew the superstitious dread which even converted natives are apt to entertain for the idols of their fathers, and the unwillingness they usually have to lay violent hands on them. He did not expect anything more than that they might permit him to remove one of the images for himself. But at this point Ramudu, the old man whose sight had been restored, stepped forward and said, "I'll bring out the chief Swami for you"; and going into the shrine he shook the biggest idol from the plaster with which it was fastened to the stone platform, and then handed it to the doctor, saying as he did so something like this :—

"Well, old fellow, be off with you! We and our ancestors for a thousand years have feared and worshipped you. Now we have found a better God, and are done with you. Be off with you, and a good riddance to us. Jesus is now our God and Saviour."

And so the ugly stone Swami that had lorded it so long over the consciences of these Telugu villagers was "dethroned," as Dr. Chamberlain puts it, "by the surgeon's knife," and passed in due course to a missionary museum in the United States. But Yesu Kristu, the Divine Guru, reigned in its stead.

But now let us follow the doctor in some of the more striking episodes of one of his earliest tours. It was a journey of 1200 miles, through the native kingdom of Hyderabad and on into Central India—a region where at that time no missionary had ever worked before. He rode all the way on a sturdy native pony, but was accompanied by four Indian assistants, with two bullock-carts full of Gospels and other Christian literature which he hoped to sell to the people at low prices.

One of their first and most dangerous adventures was in a walled city of Hyderabad. They had already disposed of a few Gospels and tracts when some Brahman priests and Mohammedan fanatics raised the mob against them. It was done in this way. A number of the Gospels were bound in cloth boards of a buff colour. The Mohammedan zealots spread a rumour that these books were bound in pig-skin — a thing which no true disciple of Mahomet will touch. The Brahmans, on the other hand, told their followers that these yellow boards were made of calf-skin—and to a Hindu the cow is a sacred animal. The crowd got thoroughly excited, and soon Dr. Chamberlain and his four helpers were standing in the market-place with their backs to a wall, while a howling multitude surged in front, many of whom had already begun to tear up the cobble-stones with which the street was paved in order to stone the intruders to death. The doctor saved the situation by getting permission to tell a wonderful story. Nothing catches an Indian crowd like the promise of a story. Their curiosity was aroused from the first, and soon their hearts were touched as they listened to a simple and graphic description of the death of Jesus on the cross. The stones dropped from the hands that clutched them, tears stood in many eyes, and when the speaker had finished every copy of the Gospels which had been brought into the city from the little camp without the walls was eagerly bought up by priests as well as people.

But dangers of this sort were rare. For the most part, both in town and country, the white traveller was welcomed courteously, and gladly listened to as he stood in the busy market-place or sat beside the village elders on the stone seat beneath the "Council-tree," and explained the purpose of his coming. Dangers of another kind, however, were common enough, and Dr. Chamberlain tells of some narrow escapes from serpents, tigers, and the other perils of the Indian jungle.

They were passing through the great teak

forest, where the trees towered one hundred and fifty feet above their heads, when they came in sight one day of a large village in a forest clearing. As they drew near, the elders of the place came out to salute them. The doctor asked if they could give him a suitable place to pitch his tent, but they did better than that, for they gave him the free use of a newly erected shed.

Somewhat tired out with a long forenoon's march, Dr. Chamberlain lay down to rest his limbs, and took up his Greek Testament meanwhile to read a chapter, holding the book over his face as he lay stretched out on his back. By and by he let his arm fall, and suddenly became aware that a huge serpent was coiled on one of the bamboo rafters just above him, and that it had gradually been letting itself down until some four feet of its body were hanging directly over his head, while its tongue was already forked out—a sure sign that it was just about to strike. He says that when studying the anatomy of the human frame he had sometimes wondered whether a person lying on his back could jump sideways, without first erecting himself, and that he discovered on this occasion that, with a proper incentive, the thing could be done.

Bounding from his dangerous position, he ran to the door of the shed and took from the bullock-cart which was standing there a huge iron spit five or six feet long, which was made for roasting meat in a jungle camp. With this as a spear he attacked the serpent, and was successful at his first thrust in pinning it to the rafter round which it was coiled. Holding the spit firmly in its place to prevent the struggling animal from shaking it out, though he ran the utmost risk of being struck as it shot out its fanged mouth in its efforts to reach his hand, he called loudly to his servant to bring him a bamboo cane. The cane was quickly brought, and then, still holding the spit in position with one hand, he beat the brute about the head till life was extinct. When quite sure that it was dead, he drew the spit out of the rafter and held it at arm's length on a level with his shoulder, the transfixed reptile hanging from it. He found that both the head and the tail touched the ground, thus showing that the serpent was not less than ten feet long.

Just at that moment the village watchman looked in at the door, and then passed on quickly into the village. And immediately it flashed into the doctor's mind that he had got himself into trouble, for he knew that these people worship serpents as gods. They never dare to kill one, and if they see a stranger trying to do so, will intercede for its life.

He was still considering what to do when he saw the chief men of the village advancing, and noticed, to his surprise, that they were carrying brass trays in their hands covered with sweetmeats, cocoanuts, and limes. His surprise was greater still when, as they reached the doorway in which he stood to meet them, they bowed down before him to the ground and presented their simple offerings, hailing him at the same time as the deliverer of their village. That deadly serpent, they told him, had been the terror of the place for several years. It had killed a child and several of their cattle, but they had never ventured to attack it, for they knew that if any of them did so he would be accursed. The kindred of the dead serpent would wage war upon that man and his family, until every one of them was exterminated. But their visitor had killed it without their knowledge or consent, and so they were freed from the pest of their lives, and at the same time were absolutely guiltless of its blood. Their gratitude knew no bounds. They pressed upon the doctor the fattest sheep in their flocks. They sent the village crier with his tom-tom all round the place to summon the people to come and hear the words of "the serpent-destroyer." And when Dr. Chamberlain seized the opportunity to speak to them about "that old serpent called the devil," and One who came to bruise the serpent's head, they listened to him as he had rarely been listened to before.

While serpents were, and still are, the most frequent danger of the traveller in the jungle, tigers were very numerous in the Telugu country forty years ago. Dr. Chamberlain has stories to tell both of the striped tiger, the royal tiger as it is commonly called, and the

ATTACKED BY A TIGER, WITH NO WEAPON BUT AN UMBRELLA

Dr. Chamberlain came face to face with a spotted tiger in a lonely mountain path, he had no weapon, but emitting a Red Indian war-whoop and suddenly putting up his umbrella, he put the animal to flight.

smaller spotted variety, which is marked like a leopard, but has a tiger's claws and cannot climb trees as a leopard can. On one occasion, when all alone and unarmed, he met a spotted tiger face to face on a narrow mountain path, but succeeded in putting the beast to flight by suddenly opening his big white umbrella and letting out a Red Indian war-whoop which he had learned when a boy from a tribe of American Indians in Michigan. An experience with a tiger of the larger sort, however, though less dramatic, was probably a good deal more dangerous.

It was about three weeks after their narrow escape from stoning in that walled city of Hyderabad, and they were still in the territories of the Nizam, but about one hundred miles farther north and in the midst of hill and jungle. The native assistants with the servants and bullock-carts had made an earlier start, and the doctor was riding on to overtake them when he noticed in the path, and side by side with the fresh cart tracks, the footprints of a huge tiger and its cub. He had been warned before plunging into the forest that seven people had recently been killed in this very neighbourhood by man-eating tigers; and it seemed evident that this tiger was following the carts with murderous intent. It is not the way of a tiger to attack a group of travellers. It watches and waits until one of them falls behind or gets detached from the rest, and then it makes its spring. Dr. Chamberlain realized the situation at once. The little caravan was safe so long as all kept close together, but if any one lagged behind the others, or stopped to quench his thirst at the wayside stream, the tiger would be on him in a moment.

Pulling out a loaded fourteen-inch Navy revolver, the only weapon he carried with him in his expeditions through the jungle, and dashing his spurs into his pony, he galloped on through the forest to warn those ahead. As he flew onwards his eye was on the path, and always he saw the cart tracks and the footprints of the tiger side by side. A deadly fear took hold of him that he might be too late. But suddenly there came a turn in the road, and there, not far in front, were the two carts and their attendants moving slowly and peacefully forward. And now the doctor noticed that the tiger tracks were gone. He had seen them last at the very corner round which the carts came into sight. Hearing the sharp tattoo of the pony's hoofs coming up behind, the tiger must have leaped into the bushes at that very point. Probably it was only a few feet from the horseman as he whisked past. But either his sudden appearance on his galloping steed gave it a fright, or else his motion was too rapid to offer the chance of a successful spring.

Not the least of the difficulties of travel in the wild parts of India is caused by the tropical floods. On one occasion Dr. Chamberlain and his little band were swept bodily down a river, usually fordable, but swollen now by recent rains. For a moment or two the doctor and his pony were submerged, but ultimately the whole company managed to swim or scramble safely to the opposite bank.

But it was a flood on the great Godavery river and its affluents that caused the worst predicament of all. By that time they had reached the extreme point of the expedition, up among the mountain Gonds, and had turned to the south-east to make the return journey by a different route. At a certain point they found that the steamer on which they had counted had broken down in attempting to stem the furious current, and that there was nothing for it but to march through seventy-five miles of a jungly, fever-haunted swamp in order to reach another steamer lower down. Bullock-carts were of no use, but by the aid of a *hookam* or firman from the Nizam himself which the doctor had got hold of, he succeeded in obtaining a large body of bearers from a native deputy-governor. These men, however, though promised threefold wages, were most unwilling to accompany him, for with the country in flood the jungle becomes a place of special dangers; and it was only by much flourishing of the aforesaid Navy pistol, though without any intention of using it, that the doctor could make his men march at all or keep them from deserting.

But by and by an unforeseen trouble emerged.

The constant dripping rain, the steamy heat, the jungle fever, the prowling tigers had all been taken into account. What had not been realized was the exceptional violence of the floods. And so one evening, when they came to a little tributary of the Godavery which must be crossed if they were to reach a place of safety for the night, they found that the back-water of the main stream, rushing up this channel, had made a passage absolutely impossible.

For a time they were almost at their wits' end, for it would have been almost as much as their lives were worth to spend the night in the midst of the swamp, and it was too late now to get back to the place from which they had started that morning. But guidance came in answer to prayer. Dr. Chamberlain tells us that all at once he seemed to hear a voice saying, "Turn to the left of the Godavery, and you will find rescue." And though the native guides assured him that to do so would only be a foolish waste of time and strength, as the Godavery was now a swirling flood three miles across, and no boat or raft could possibly be got within a distance of many miles, he made his men turn sharp to the left and march in the direction of the Godavery bank. To his great delight, and to the astonishment of the natives, the first thing they saw as they emerged from the bushes was a large flat boat, just at their feet, fastened to a tree on the shore.

The boatmen told them that early that morning their cables had snapped, and they had been carried away by the flood from a mooring station higher upstream and on the British side of the river. To this precise spot they had been swept, they could not tell how. But to Dr. Chamberlain and his four native evangelists it seemed clear that God had sent this boat expressly for their deliverance. They pitched their tent on the broad deck, and kindled a large fire on the shore to keep wild beasts away. And though the tigers scented them, and could be heard growling and snarling in the bushes that fringed the bank, the night was passed in comparative comfort and safety. Next day they floated down the stream towards the steamer that was to carry them southwards. And so ended the more adventurous part of this long missionary journey through the country of the Telugus.

NOTE.—The material for this chapter is derived from Dr. Chamberlain's two books already referred to, *The Cobra's Den* and *In the Tiger Jungle*, both published by Messrs. Oliphant, Anderson, and Ferrier.

A JAPANESE ROMANCE

CHAPTER III

A JAPANESE ROMANCE

Romantic Japan—The *daimio* and the stable-boy—Thirsting for truth—In a junk to Hakodate—A schooner and a stowaway—A discovery in Hong-Kong—Arrival in Boston—Mr. Hardy and "Joe"—At Amherst and Andover—The Mikado's embassy—Neesima's educational dreams—Return to Japan—The "Doshisha"—The wooden cross and the living monument.

THERE is no country on the map of the world with which it is more natural to associate the idea of romance than the island empire of Japan. The sudden awaking of the people from their sleep of centuries, their transition in the course of a single generation from something like European medievalism to the most up-to-date modernity, may fairly be described as one of the greatest wonders of history. Heroic as well as romantic, recalling twice over the immortal story of David and Goliath, are the two wars which the little Power has waged triumphantly in quick succession against the biggest empires—first of Asia and then of Europe. Romantic, too, as every traveller tells us, are the sights of the country and the ways of the people wherever Old Japan survives—the houses, the gardens, the elaborate courtesies, the artistic costumes, the combination of a frank naturalism with an artificiality which has become a second nature. In reading about Japan we sometimes feel as if we had to do not with the world of sober realities, but with a fascinating chapter out of a new volume of *Arabian Nights*. And yet even in a land in which wonders meet us on every side, the strange story of Joseph Neesima deserves to be called romantic.

He was born in 1843. It was ten years before that memorable Sabbath morning when Commodore Perry, of the U.S. Navy, with his fleet of "barbarian" ships steamed into the harbour of Uraga, in the Bay of Yedo, and extorted from a reluctant Government those treaties of friendship and commerce which broke down for ever the walls of seclusion behind which Japan had hid herself from the eyes of the world. Neesima was a *samurai*, a member of the old fighting caste of feudal times, and so even as

PRAYING TO IDOLS

A Japanese peasant girl saying her prayers to the stone images of Amida. The load on her back is firewood.

a boy wore a sword and was sworn to a life of fealty to the *daimio* or prince on whose estate he was born.

From the first, however, it was evident that this little serf had a mind and will of his own, and also a passionate longing for truth and freedom. He devoted all his spare time to study, often sitting up over his books until the morning cocks began to crow. Once the prince, his master, caught him running away from his ordinary duties to go to the house of a teacher whom he was in the habit of visiting by stealth. After giving the boy a severe flogging, he asked him where he was going. Neesima's answer will best be given in his own words at a time when he had learned only enough English to write it in the "pidgin" fashion. "'Why you run out from here?' the *daimio* said. Then I answered him, 'That I wish to learn foreign knowledge, because foreigners have got best knowledge, and I hope to understand very quickly.' Then he said, 'With what reason will you like foreign knowledge? Perhaps it will mistake yourself.' I said to him sooner, 'Why will it mistake myself? I guess every one must take some knowledge. If a man has not any knowledge, I will worth him as a dog or a pig.' Then he laughed, and said to me, 'You are a stable-boy.'"

Not less remarkable than this thirst for knowledge was the lad's consciousness of the rights of human beings, and passionate desire for fuller liberty: "A day my comrade sent me a Atlas of United States, which was written in Chinese letter by some American minister. I read it many times, and was wondered so much as my brain would melted out of my head, because I liked it very much—picking one President, building free schools, poor-houses, house of correction, and machine-working, and so forth, and thought that a government of every country must be as President of United States. And I murmured myself that, O governor of Japan! why you keep down us, as a dog or a pig? We are people of Japan; if you govern us, you must love us as your children."

But above all young Neesima felt a deep longing after God. When he was about fifteen years of age, to the great distress of his relatives, he refused to worship any longer the family gods which stood on a shelf in the house. He saw for himself that they were "only whittled things," and that they never touched the food and drink which he offered to them. Not long after this he got possession of an abridged Bible history in the Chinese language, with which he was well acquainted, and was immensely struck by the opening sentence, "In the beginning God created the heaven and the earth." Immediately he recognized the Creator's claim to be worshipped. To this still Unknown God he began thereafter to pray, "Oh, if You have eyes, look upon me; if You have ears, listen for me."

Before long it became Neesima's constant desire to find his way to the port of Hakodate, as an open port, where he thought he might fall in with some Englishman or American from whom to obtain the knowledge that he wanted. He made application to the *daimio* to be allowed to undertake the voyage, but got only a scolding and a beating for his pains. Yet he did not despair. In the quaint language of his earliest English style, "My stableness did not destroy by their expostulalations." He waited patiently for four or five years, and at last, to his inexpressible joy, secured permission to go to Hakodate in a sailing-junk which belonged to his master. The junk was a coaster, and it was several weeks before he reached the haven of his hopes. Getting to Hakodate at last, it seemed for a time as if nothing but disappointment was in store for him there. He could find no one to teach him English, and meanwhile his little stock of money melted rapidly away. At length matters began to look brighter. He fell in with a Russian priest who gave him some employment, and he made the acquaintance of a young Jap, Mr. Munokite, who was a clerk in an English store, and who not only taught him a little English, but helped to carry out a secret determination he had now formed of escaping to America at the earliest opportunity.

He had not come to this decision without long and anxious thought. It involved great sacrifices and no small danger. In those days a Japanese subject was forbidden to leave the country on pain of death. If caught in the act of attempting to do so, he forfeited his life; while if he made good his escape, this meant that he had banished himself for ever from the "Land of the Rising Sun."

It was painful for the youth to think of leaving his parents without even saying good-bye, and with no prospect of ever seeing them again, especially as he had been brought up under the influence of the Confucian doctrine of filial obedience. But he thought the matter out, and saw at last that in the search for truth and God it may be proper to set all other claims aside. "I discovered for the first time," he wrote afterwards, "that the doctrines of Confucius on the filial relations are narrow and fallacious. I felt that I must take my own course. I must serve my Heavenly Father more than my earthly parents."

And Neesima loved his country as well as his home, for patriotism is a sentiment which glows with extraordinary warmth in every Japanese heart. Moreover, he was something of a poet as well as a patriot, seeing his country in the glowing hues of a lively imagination. The verses he wrote far out on the China Sea, after he had made good his flight, show how his heart kept turning back to the dear land of flowers. "If a man be determined in his mind to run away a thousand miles," one of his poems says, "he expects to have to endure great sufferings, and why can he be anxious about his home? But how strange! In the night, when the spring wind is blowing, in a dream he sees flowers in the garden at home."

But we are anticipating somewhat, for the story of Neesima's adventurous flight has yet to be told. After endless difficulties, his friend Munokite secured leave for him to work his passage to Shanghai on an American schooner, the *Berlin*, Captain Savory. He had, of course, to smuggle himself on board at his own risk, and to do so with the full knowledge that if detected by the harbour police he would be handed over to the executioner without delay. His plans had accordingly to be laid with the utmost caution. When night fell, he had a secret meeting in a private house with Munokite and two other young friends. They supped together, and passed round the *sake*-

cup in token of love and faithfulness. At midnight the fugitive crept out of the house in the garb of a servant, carrying a bundle and following one of his friends who walked in front with a dignified air wearing two swords, as if he were the master. By back streets and dark lanes they found their way to the water's edge, where a small boat was already in waiting. Neesima was placed in the bottom of the boat and covered up with a tarpaulin as if he were a cargo of provisions; and then swiftly, but with muffled oars, the boatman pulled out to the schooner. A rope was thrown over the side, and the cargo, suddenly becoming very much alive, scrambled on board and hurried below.

That night he never slept a wink, for he knew that the worst danger was yet to come. In those days every vessel leaving Hakodate harbour was keenly searched at the last moment to make sure that no Japanese subject was secreted anywhere on board. Early next morning the police boat was seen coming off to the schooner for this purpose; and Neesima felt that his hour of destiny was at hand. But Captain Savory had laid his plans carefully too, for he also was running a risk; and he hid his dangerous passenger in a part of the ship where the watch-dogs of the port never thought of looking for him. The search was over at last; the anchor weighed; the sails spread to an off-shore breeze. The *Berlin* forged her way through the shipping and out to the open sea. Neesima was now safe and free. It was on 18 July, 1864, and the hero of our story was twenty-one years of age.

After a very disagreeable passage to Shanghai and ten days of wretchedness and uncertainty in that busy port, where he could not get rid of the idea that even yet he might be betrayed and sent back to Japan, our adventurer found another American vessel, the *Wild Rover*, bound for Boston, and succeeded in persuading the captain to take him on board without wages as his own personal servant. The voyage was a tedious one, for the *Wild Rover* was a "tramp," which sailed here and there about the China seas for eight months before turning homewards, and spent four months more on the ocean passage. While they were lying in Hong-Kong harbour Neesima discovered a Chinese

New Testament in a shop, and felt that he must secure it at all costs. But he had not a copper of his own, and having promised to work his passage without wages, felt that he could not ask the captain for any money. At last he bethought himself of his sword, which, being a *samurai*, he had brought with him as a matter of course. Could he honourably part with this weapon which marked the dignity of his caste, and was to him like his shield to a young Spartan—an indispensable badge of his own self-respect? He was not long in deciding. The Japanese sword was soon in the hands of a dealer, and Neesima triumphantly bore his prize back to the ship. He read the book day and night, and found in it answers to some of the questions which had so long perplexed his mind.

When the *Wild Rover* reached Boston our hero's trials were by no means over. The Civil War had lately ended. Work was scarce; the price of everything was high. Nobody wanted this Japanese lad with his "pidgin" English and his demand to be sent to school. He began to fear that the hopes of years might only have been delusions arter all. "I could not read book very cheerfully," he remarks, "and I am only looking around myself a long time as a lunatic."

It is quite characteristic of his romantic experiences that his first real comfort came from a copy of *Robinson Crusoe* which he picked up for a few cents in a second-hand bookstore. Possibly he felt that there were some analogies between his adventures and trials and those of the hero of Defoe's great romance, and that he was almost as friendless and solitary on the shores of this great continent as the shipwrecked mariner on that lonely island beach. But what appealed to him most of all was Crusoe's prayers. Hitherto he had cried to God as an unknown God, feeling all the while that perhaps God had no eyes to see him, no ears to listen for him. Now he learned from Crusoe's manner of praying that in all his troubles he must cry to God as a present, personal friend. And so day by day, in the full belief that God was listening, he uttered this prayer: "Please don't cast me away into miserable condition. Please let me reach my great aim."

Neesima's worst anxieties were nearly over now. His "great aim" was almost in sight. As soon as the *Wild Rover* reached Boston, the captain had gone off on a long visit to his friends, not thinking much about his Japanese cabin-boy or expecting to see him again. But on his return to his ship some weeks after, he found "Joe," as the lad was called on shipboard, still hovering about the vessel as his one ark of refuge. This led him to speak to his owner, a Mr. Hardy, of the queer young Oriental he had brought to America; and Mr. Hardy, who was a large-hearted and generous Christian man, at once declared that he would make some provision for the poor fellow. His first idea was to employ him as a house servant; but when his wife and he met the youth and heard his wonderful story, they saw immediately that this was no ordinary immigrant of the stowaway order; and instead of making him a servant they took him into their family practically as an adopted son, and gave him a thorough education, first in an academy at Andover and afterwards at Amherst College. It was in token of this adoption that, when he was baptized as a member of the Christian Church, he took his full name of Joseph Hardy Neesima. On shipboard, as has been mentioned, he was called "Joe," the sailors having decided that he must have some short and handy name, and "Joe" suggesting itself as convenient. "Keep the name," Mr. Hardy said after hearing how it was given. For he felt that, like another Joseph, who went down to Egypt as a captive and became the saviour of his brethren, Joseph Neesima, the Japanese runaway, might yet become a benefactor to his country. He lived long enough to see his hopes much more than realized.

After graduating honourably at Amherst College, Neesima entered himself a student at Andover Theological Seminary, with the view of being ordained as a fully qualified missionary to his own countrymen. Soon after this a pathway for his return to Japan opened up in a manner which was almost dramatic. Since his departure from Hakodate in 1864, the chariot wheels of progress had been moving rapidly in the land of his birth. Japan was beginning to deserve in a wider sense than before its name of "The Land of the Rising Sun." Instead of closing all her doors and windows and endeavouring to shut out the light at every chink, she was now eager to live and move in the full sunshine of Western knowledge. The great political and social revolution had taken place. The Mikado had issued that epoch-making proclamation in which he declared: "The uncivilized customs of former times will be broken; the impartiality and justice displayed in the workings of nature adopted as a basis of action; and intellect and learning will be sought for throughout the world in order to establish the foundations of empire."

It was in pursuance of this new policy that there came to Washington in the winter of 1871-72 a distinguished embassy from the Imperial Court of Japan, which had for its special commission to inspect and report upon the workings of Western civilization. The embassy soon felt the need of some one who could not only act as intrepreter, but assist it in the task of examining the institutions, and especially the educational institutions, of foreign lands. For some time Mr. Mori, the

Japanese Minister in the United States, had had his eye on his young countryman at Andover, and he now invited him to Washington to be introduced to the embassy. So favourable was the impression produced by his personal appearance, and so evident was it that he was thoroughly conversant with the principles and methods of Western culture, that he was immediately requested to accompany the ambassadors in the capacity of adviser, on their tour through the United States and Europe; while overtures of the most flattering kind were made to him, with brilliant prospects in the political world whenever he returned to his native land. But Neesima's mind was now fully made up regarding his work in life. When he returned to Japan it would be not as a politician, but as a Christian missionary. In the meantime, however, he willingly put his services at the disposal of the Mikado's embassy, and thereby not only greatly enlarged his experience, but gained influential friends among the rising statesmen of Japan, friends who were afterwards of no small help to him in his effort to promote among his countrymen the cause of Christian civilization. The special task was assigned to him of drawing up a paper on "The Universal Education of Japan." He discharged the duty with such ability that his essay became the basis of the report subsequently made by the embassy on the subject of education. And this report, with certain modifications, was the foundation of the Japanese system of education as it has existed ever since.

After a year had been spent in this interesting way, Neesima returned to Andover, and on the completion of his theological course was ordained by the American Board of Missions as an evangelist to his fellow-countrymen, his foster-father, Mr. Hardy, undertaking to provide for his support. Ten years had now elapsed from the time when he was smuggled out of Japan in the hold of a little schooner—a poor and unknown lad, and a criminal in the eyes of the law. He was about to return a highly cultured Christian gentleman, with not a few influential friends on both sides of the Pacific. And he was returning with a purpose. He had found the light he came to seek, but he was far from being satisfied with that. His aim now was to be a light-bringer to Japan. He was deeply conscious of the truth that

> Heaven doth with us as we with torches do,
> Not light them for themselves.

He was unwilling, says Dr. Davis, his colleague in after years and one of his biographers, "to go back with a full heart but with an empty hand." His purpose was to start a Christian College in which he could meet the craving of young Japan for Western knowledge —the craving which he knew so well—while at the same time he might surround the students with a Christian atmosphere, and train some of them to be preachers and teachers of Jesus Christ. But he could not start a college without means, and where the means were to come from he did not know.

He spoke of his plans in the first place to various members of the American Board. But the Board's hands were full, and he met with no encouragement. Then he took counsel with himself. It had been arranged that before leaving America he should give an address at the annual public meeting of the Board, and he determined to utilize this opportunity. To the very best of his ability he prepared a speech. But when he stepped on to the platform and faced the great audience, a fate befell him which has often come to public speakers at a critical moment in the beginning of their careers. His carefully arranged ideas all disappeared; his mind became a perfect blank; and every one present thought that he had completely broken down. But suddenly a thought flashed into his mind, opening up an entirely fresh line of address, and for fifteen minutes, while the tears streamed down his cheeks, he pleaded the cause of his country with such overwhelming earnestness that at the close of his short speech 5000 dollars were subscribed on the spot, and Neesima knew that the foundation-stone of a Christian College in Japan was already laid.

It was characteristic of our hero's indomitable courage that when he reached Japan he started his college, which he called the "Doshisha," or "Company of One Endeavour" — not in any city of the coast, where Western ideas had become familiar, but in

Kyoto itself, the sacred city of the interior, a city of 6000 temples and the very heart of the religious life of Old Japan. In this place, where Buddhism and Shintoism had flourished unchallenged for a thousand years, Neesima was subjected for a time to the furious hatred of the native priests and even to the opposition of the magistrates. For the most part these men had no objections to Western education, but Christian education they would have liked to suppress. It was now that he realized the advantage of the friendship of the members of the embassy of 1871–2. Several of those gentlemen, including the present Marquis Ito, had become prominent members of the Japanese Cabinet, and they did not a little to remove difficulties out of Neesima's way.

And so the Doshisha took root and flourished, until in the last year of its founder's life, when he had been engaged in his work for fifteen years, the number of students in all departments, young women as well as young men, had risen to over 900. Neesima wore himself out by his labours, and died at the comparatively early age of 47, just when he had taken steps to broaden out the Doshisha College into the Doshisha University, and had secured large sums for this purpose, including a single gift of 100,000 dollars from a gentleman in New England, and a collection of 31,000 yen subscribed at a dinner-party in Tokyo in the house of Count Inouye, after those present had been addressed by Neesima himself, who was one of the guests.

Neesima's widow has fulfilled his last wish, spoken from the depths of a humble Christian heart: "Raise no monument after my death. It is enough, if on a wooden cross there stand the words, 'the grave of Joseph Neesima.'" But the Doshisha is Neesima's living monument in Japan. More than 5000 students have passed through it, of whom in 1903 above eighty were preachers of the Gospel, 161 were teachers, 27 were Government officials, and 16 were newspaper editors. By turning out a succession of highly educated men and women trained under Christian influences, Neesima's college has contributed no small part in the creation of that New Japan which has so swiftly stepped in these late years into the foremost rank of the great company of nations.

The chief authority for this chapter is *A Maker of New Japan: Joseph Hardy Neesima*, by Rev. J. D. Davis, D.D. (Fleming H. Revell Co.)

"FROM FAR FORMOSA"

CHAPTER IV

"FROM FAR FORMOSA"

George Leslie Mackay—A lawless land—The Malay and the Chinaman—Dentistry and the Gospel—A cruel plot—The capture of Bang-kah—The barbarians of the plain—The Kap-tsu-lan fishermen—The mountain head-hunters—A Christmas night in a head-hunter's house.

FOR the title of this chapter we have taken the name of a book by Dr. George Leslie Mackay, of the Canadian Presbyterian Church, whose acquaintance with Formosa and its people—the people of the mountains as well as of the plains—is of an altogether unique kind. The title is appropriate, for though on the map Formosa is not more distant than China or Japan, it is much farther off than the moon to the vast majority of people, so far as any knowledge of it is concerned. Indeed, until it became a storm centre of the Chino-Japanese War of 1895, and passed under the sway of the Mikado, and was thus made an object of fresh interest to the Western world, there were numbers of fairly well-informed people who knew no more about it than that it was an island somewhere in the Eastern Seas. But more than thirty years ago it had attracted the attention of Mr. Mackay, a young Canadian of Highland Scottish descent. Sent out to China as a missionary by the Presbyterian Church of Canada, which gave him a pretty free hand in the selection of a definite sphere, he chose the northern part of Formosa—perfectly virgin soil so far as any Christian work was concerned. The evangelization of North Formosa was a hard and dangerous task to be attempted by a single man, but Mackay flung himself into it with all the enthusiasm of a Celt, as well as the steady devotion of a brave soldier of the Church militant.

Formosa was a wild and lawless land, with its mixture of mutually hostile races, its debased Mongolians and savage Malayans, its men of the plains and men of the mountains, its corrupt officials in the towns and savage head-hunters in the hill forests. Mackay, however, went about fearlessly, with a dentist's forceps (a wonderful talisman) in one hand and a Bible in the other. At one time we find him sleeping contentedly in the filthy cabin of a farmer on the swampy rice plains with a litter of pigs, it might almost be said, for his bed-fellows, the pig being a highly domesticated animal in Formosa, and treated by its master as an Englishman treats his pet dog. Again, he is far up amongst the mountains in the land of the head-hunters, where his sleeping apartment, which is also the sleeping apartment of the whole family, is adorned with a row of grinning skulls and queues that testifies to the prowess of his host in murdering Chinamen and other dwellers on the plains. It was by a courage and persistence which nothing could daunt that this young Scoto-Canadian won his way in Formosa, until to those who are interested in the history of missions, "Mackay of Formosa" seems as natural and inevitable a title as "Mackay of Uganda" or "Chalmers of New Guinea."

Apart from the Japanese settlers who have planted themselves in the island since the war of 1895, the population of Formosa is divided between the aborigines, who are of a Malayan stock, and the Chinese, who in ever-increasing numbers have poured in from the adjacent mainland. Though only half the size of Scotland, the island is dominated by a range of mountains quite Alpine in their height, the loftiest rising to between 14,000 and 15,000 feet above the sea. Along the coast, however, there are fertile stretches, perfectly flat, formed by the alluvial deposits washed down in the course of ages. On the richer of these plains, as well as on the lower reaches of the hills, the incoming Chinamen settled, usually by no better title than the right of might. "Rice-farms and tea-plantations took the place of forest tangle and wild plateau; the rude hamlets of another race vanished; towns and cities with their unmistakable marks of the 'Middle Kingdom' took their place; and the Chinese became a superior power in Formosa."

To the Chinese, of course, the original inhabitants without exception were "barbarians," but the Malayan population, though comprising a great many different tribes, may be roughly divided into two well-defined sections.

First there are those who have accepted Chinese authority, and in a modified form have adopted the Chinese civilization and religion. These go by the name of Pe-po-hoan, or "barbarians of the plain." Then there are those who have absolutely refused to acknowledge the Chinese invaders as the masters of Formosa, and, though driven into the mountains and forests, have retained their ancestral freedom. These are the much-dreaded Chhi-hoan or "raw barbarians," whose manner of life in many respects recalls that of their kinsmen the Hill Dyaks of Borneo. Among these mountain savages, as formerly among the Dyaks, head-hunting is cultivated as a fine art. They hate the Chinese with a deadly hatred, and hardly less their own Pe-po-hoan kinsfolk who have yielded to the stranger and accepted his ways. Pe-po-hoan and Chinaman alike are considered as fair game, and their skulls are mingled indiscriminately in the ghastly collection which is the chief glory of the mountain brave, as it forms the principal adornment of his dwelling.

Naturally it was among the Chinese in the towns that Mackay began his work. He was fortunate in gathering round him very early some earnest young men, who not only accepted Christianity for themselves, but became his disciples and followers with a view to teaching and helping others. These students, as they were called, accompanied him on all his tours, not only gaining valuable experience thereby, but being of real assistance in various ways. For instance, Mackay soon discovered that the people of Formosa, partly because of the prevalence of malarial fever, and partly because they are constantly chewing the betel-nut, have very rotten teeth and suffer dreadfully from toothache. Though not a doctor, he knew a little of medicine and surgery, having attended classes in these subjects by way of preparing himself for his work abroad; but he found that nothing helped him so much in making his way among the people as his modest skill in dentistry. The priests and other enemies of Christianity might persuade the people that their fevers and other ailments had been cured not by the medicines of the "foreign devil," but by the intervention of their own gods. The power of the missionary,

Dr. MacKay and his Assistants as Dentists

The practice of dentistry in Formosa was found to be a great help in getting into touch with the natives.

however, to give instantaneous relief to one in the agonies of toothache was unmistakable, and tooth-extraction worked wonders in breaking down prejudice and opposition. It was here that some of the students proved especially useful. They learned to draw teeth almost if not quite as well as Mackay himself, so that between them they were able to dispose of as many as 500 patients in an afternoon.

The usual custom of Mackay and his little band of students as they journeyed about the country was to take their stand in an open space, often on the stone steps of a temple, and after singing a hymn or two to attract attention, to proceed to the work of tooth-pulling, thereafter inviting the people to listen to their message. For the most part the crowd was very willing to listen. Sudden relief from pain produces gratitude even towards a "foreign devil," and the innate Chinese suspicion of some black arts or other evil designs was always guarded against by scrupulously placing the tooth of each patient in the palm of his own hand. The people began to love

Mackay, and this opened their hearts to his preaching. Men and women came to confess their faith, and in one large village which was the centre of operations there were so many converts that a preaching-hall had to be secured, which Sunday after Sunday was packed by an expectant crowd.

Opposition is often the best proof of success, and in Mackay's case it soon came in cruel and tragic forms. A cunning plot was laid between the priestly party and the civil officials to accuse a number of these Chinese Christians of conspiring to assassinate the mandarin. Six innocent men were seized and put in the stocks in the dungeons of the city of Bang-kah. Mock trials were held, in the course of which the prisoners were bambooed, made to kneel on red-hot chains, and tortured in various other ways. At last one morning two of the heroic band, a father and son, were taken out of their dungeon and dragged off to the place of execution. The son's head was chopped off before his father's eyes, after which the old man too was put to death. Then their heads, placed in baskets, were carried slowly back to

Bang-kah with the notice fixed above them, *Jip kon-e lang than* ("Heads of the Christians"). All along the way the town-crier summoned the multitude to witness the fate of those who followed the "barbarian." And when the walls of Bang-kah were reached the two heads were fastened above the city gate, just as the heads of criminals or martyrs used to be set above the Netherbow at Edinburgh or Temple Bar in London, for a terror and a warning to all who passed by. It was a cruel fate, and yet better than that of the remaining prisoners. Their lot was to be slowly starved or tortured to death in their filthy dungeons.

But in spite of these horrors—partly, we might say, because of them—the number of Christians in North Formosa steadily grew, until at length, as Dr. Mackay puts it, "Bang-kah itself was taken." Not that this important place, "the Gibraltar of heathendom" in the island, was transformed into a Christian city. But it ceased, at all events, to be fiercely anti-Christian, and came to honour the very man whom it had hustled, hooted at, pelted with mud and rotten eggs, and often plotted to kill. A striking proof of the change was given by and by when Mackay was about to return to Canada on a visit. The head men of the city sent a deputation to ask him to allow them to show their appreciation of himself and his work by according him a public send-off. He was not sure about it at first, not caring much for demonstrations of this kind, but on reflection concluded that it might be well, and might do good to the Christian cause, to allow them to have their own way. So he was carried through the streets of Bang-kah to the jetty in a silk-lined sedan-chair, preceded by the officials of the place, and followed by three hundred soldiers and bands of civilians bearing flags and banners, to a musical accompaniment provided by no fewer than eight Chinese orchestras made up of cymbals, drums, gongs, pipes, guitars, mandolines, tambourines, and clarionets. Heathens and Christians alike cheered him as he boarded the steam-launch which was to take him off from the shore, while the Christians who had stood firmly by him through troublous times broke into a Chinese version of the old Scottish paraphrase, "I'm not ashamed to own my Lord."

But while Mackay found his base of operations among the Chinese in the north and west of Formosa, he did not forget the Malayan aborigines, whether those of the plains or those of the mountains. As soon as he had got a firm footing and gathered a band of competent helpers around him, he began to turn his attention to the Pe-po-hoan, the "barbarians of the plain," who cultivate their rice-farms in the low-lying and malarial districts along the north-east coast. He had already experienced many of the drawbacks of Formosan travel. He had known what it was to be swept down the current in trying to ford dangerous streams, to push his way through jungles full of lurking serpents, to encounter hostile crowds in village or town who jeered at the "foreign devil," or regarded him, as the boy said of birds in his essay on the subject, as being "very useful to throw stones at." And night when it came he had often found not less trying than day, possibly still more so. The filthy rest-houses were not places of much rest to a white man. Pigs frisked out and in, and slept or grunted beneath the traveller's bed. The bed itself was a plank with brick legs, the mattress a dirty grass mat on which coolies had smoked opium for years. And when, overpowered by weariness, he fell asleep, he was apt to be suddenly awakened by the attacks of what he humorously describes as "three generations of crawling creatures."

Greater dangers and worse discomforts than these, however, had now to be faced in carrying the Gospel to the country of the Pe-po-hoan. In the mountains over which it was necessary to pass in order to cross from the west coast to the east, Mackay and his students had to run the gauntlet of the stealthy head-hunters. They had more than one narrow escape. Passing by the mouth of a gorge one day, they heard in the distance blood-curdling yells and screams, and presently a Chinese came rushing up all out of breath and told them that he and four others had just been attacked by the savages, and that his companions were all speared and beheaded, while he had only managed to escape with his life. When the plains were reached the Pe-po-hoan did not prove at first a friendly or receptive people. From village after village they were turned away with reviling, the inhabitants often setting their wolfish dogs upon them. The weather was bad, and in that low-lying region the roads were soon turned into quagmires where the feet sank into eighteen inches of mud. When night fell a Chinese inn would have been welcome enough; but sometimes no better sleeping-place could be had than the lee side of a dripping rice-stack.

But after a while things began to improve. Like Jesus in Galilee, Mackay found his first disciples in the Kap-tsu-lan plain among the fishermen — bold, hardy fellows, who live in scattered villages along that coast. Three of these fishers came to him one day and said, "You have been going through and through our plain, and no one has received you. Come to our village, and we will listen to you." They led Mackay and his students to their village, gave them a good supper of rice and fish, and then one of them took a large conch shell, which in other days had served as a war-trumpet, and summoned the whole population to an assembly. Till the small hours of the morning Mackay was kept busy preaching, conversing, discussing, and answering questions. The very next day these people determined to have a church of their own in which to worship the true God. They sailed down the coast to the forest country farther south to cut logs of wood, and though they were attacked by the savages while doing so, and some of them wounded, they returned in due course with a load of timber. Bricks were made out of mud and rice-chaff, and a primitive little chapel was soon erected, in which every evening at the blowing of the conch the entire village met to hear the preacher. Mackay stayed two months in this place, and by that time it had become nominally Christian. Several times, he tells us, he dried his dripping clothes at night in front of a fire made of idolatrous paper, idols, and ancestral tablets which the people had given him to destroy. One reason for this rapid and wholesale conversion to Christianity no doubt lay in the fact that the Chinese idolatry which these Pe-po-hoan fishermen had been induced to accept never came very near to their hearts. Originally they or their fathers had been nature-worshippers, as all the mountain savages still are, and many of them were inclined to look upon the rites and ceremonies to which they submitted as unwelcome reminders of their subjection to an alien race.

What took place in this one village was soon repeated in several others on the Kap-tsu-lan plain. Even in places where men, women, and children had rejected him at first and hurled "the contumelious stone" at his head, Mackay came to be welcomed by the people as their best friend. And by and by no fewer than nineteen chapels sprang up in that plain, the preachers and pastors in every case being native Christians, and several of them being drawn from among the Pe-po-hoan themselves.

But something must now be said about the Chhi-hoan, or savage barbarians of the mountains. More than once in the course of his tours among the Pe-po-hoan Mackay narrowly escaped from the spears and knives of these warriors, who live by hunting wild animals in the primeval forests, but whose peculiar delight it is to hunt for human heads, and above all for the heads of the hated Chinese. On one occasion a party of Chinese traders with whom he was staying in an outpost settlement was attacked by a band of two dozen savages; and though the latter were eventually beaten off, it was not till they had secured the heads of three of Mackay's trading friends.

According to the unwritten law of the mountain villages, no man is permitted to marry until he has proved his prowess by bringing at least one head to his chief, while eminence in the estimation of the tribe always depends upon the number of skulls which a brave can display under the eaves or along the inside walls of his hut. Mackay tells of one famous chief who was captured at last by the Chinese authorities, and who said, as he was led out to execution, that he was not ashamed to die, because in his house in the mountains he could show a row of skulls only six short of a hundred.

A head-hunter's outfit consists, in the first place, of a long, light thrusting-spear with an arrow-shaped blade eight inches in length. In his belt he carries a cruel-looking crooked knife

Armed Head-hunters in Formosa

Their victims are men, Chinese or even their own people who have been conquered and live amongst the Chinese. Their outfit consists of a spear, a knife, and a bag capable of holding two or three heads. No sleuth-hound is truer to the scent, no tiger stealthier of foot in the pursuit of prey.

with which to slash off his victim's head. Over the shoulder he wears a bag of strong, twisted twine, capable of carrying two or three heads at a time. From the attacks of these blood-thirsty savages none who live or move on the borderland between mountain and plain are ever secure by day or by night. In the daytime the hunters usually go out singly, concealing themselves in the tall grass of the level lands, or behind some stray boulder by a path through a glen along which sooner or later a traveller is likely to pass. When his quarry is within spear-thrust, the crouching hunter leaps upon him, striking for his heart; and soon a headless corpse is lying on the ground, while the savage, with his prize slung round his neck, is trotting swiftly, by forest paths known only to himself, towards his distant mountain home.

But more commonly the attack is made at night, and made by a party of braves. In this case everything is carefully planned for weeks before. Watchers on the hill-tops, or scouts lurking in the bush along the edge of the forests, report as to when a village festivity is likely to make its defenders less watchful, or when the fishermen have gone off on a distant fishing expedition, leaving their homes to the care of none but womenfolk. Having selected a house for attack, the savages silently surround it in the darkness, creeping stealthily nearer and nearer until, at a signal from the leader, one of them moves on before the rest and sets fire to the thatch. When the unfortunate inmates, aroused from sleep by the crackle of the flames and half-stifled by the smoke, attempt to rush out of the door, they are instantly speared and their heads secured. In a few moments, before the nearest neighbours have had time to come to the rescue, or even been awakened from their slumbers, the hunters have disappeared into the night.

The return to the village of a successful head-hunting party is a scene of fiendish delight, in which men, women, and children alike all take a part. Hour after hour dancing and drinking is carried on, as the Chhi-hoan gloat over the death of their enemies and praise the prowess of their warriors. On rare occasions the heads of the victims are boiled and the flesh eaten, but it is quite common to boil the brain to a jelly and eat it with the gusto of revenge. Dr. Mackay has himself been present in a mountain village on the return of a head-hunting party, and has been offered some of this brain jelly as a rare treat.

One who goes among such people must literally take his life in his hands, for he may at any moment fall a victim to treachery or to the inherited passion for human blood. But perfect courage and unvarying truth and kindness will carry a traveller far, and Mackay had the further advantage of being possessed of medical and surgical skill. He owed something, moreover, to his *not* having a pigtail. "You must be a kinsman of ours," the Chhi-hoan said, as they examined the missionary's back hair. And so by degrees Mackay came to live in close touch with these savages, and found that, apart from their head-hunting instincts, they had some good and amiable qualities of their own. From time to time he visited them as he got opportunity, and was even able in some cases to bring a measure of light to very benighted minds.

One year Mackay spent a Christmas holiday high up among the mountains as the guest of one of the barbarian chiefs. The house was a single large room, full thirty feet long, in which at night a fire blazed at either end. Around one fire the women squatted spinning cord for nets, around the other the braves smoked and discussed a head-hunting expedition which they proposed to undertake before long. On the walls were the customary rows of skulls, their grinning teeth lighted up fitfully by the flickering gleams from the burning fir logs. In the midst of this promiscuous crowd, which included a mother and her new-born babe, Mackay with his students had to sleep that night. But before the time came to lie down and rest, he proposed that he and his Christian companions should give a song, a proposal which secured silence at once, for the aborigines are much more musical than the Chinese, and are very fond of singing. And so on Christmas night, in that wild spot where no white man had ever been before, and to that strange audience, Mackay and his little band of Chinese converts sang some Christian hymns. And after that he told the listening savages the story of the first Christmas night, and of the love of Him who

"From Far Formosa"

was born in the stable at Bethlehem for the head-hunters of Formosa, no less than for the white men whose home was over the sea.

NOTE.—The material for this chapter is derived from Dr. Mackay's book, *From Far Formosa* (Edinburgh: Oliphant, Anderson, and Ferrier).

A HEROINE OF TIBET

CHAPTER V

A HEROINE OF TIBET

Mysterious Lhasa—The lady who tried to lift the veil—In the Himalayas—On the Chino-Tibetan frontier—The caravan for Lhasa—Attacked by brigands—The kilted Goloks—Among perpetual snows—A Tibetan love story—Noga the traitor—The arrest—Return to China—In the Chumbi Valley.

WHEN an armed British expedition struggled over the Karo-la Pass, which exceeds Mont Blanc in height, and entered Lhasa on the 3rd of August, 1904, there was a brief lifting of the veil of mystery which has hung for centuries around the city of the Grand Lama. But the wreathing snows, which began to fall so heavily around the little army before it reached the frontiers of India on the return journey, were almost symbolical of the fact that Lhasa was already wrapping herself once more in her immemorial veil of cold aloofness from European eyes. Prior to the arrival of this military expedition, only one Englishman, Thomas Manning, had succeeded in reaching

Lhasa, and it will soon be a century since his bold march was made. Sixty years ago two French missionary priests, the Abbés Huc and Gabet, undertook their celebrated journey from China to Lhasa, which they afterwards described in a very interesting book. But though they reached their goal, they gained little by it, for they were soon deported back to China again. No Protestant missionary has ever set foot in Lhasa, and what is more, no Protestant missionary, with one exception, has ever made a determined attempt to reach it. And to the honour of her sex be it said, the one who made the attempt and all but succeeded was a lady, and a lady with no other following than a couple of faithful Asiatic servants.

The character and career of Miss Annie R. Taylor remind one at some points of the late General Gordon. There is the same shrinking from public notice, the same readiness to be buried from the sight of Europe in some distant and difficult task, the same courage which fears nothing, the same simple, unquestioning trust in the care and guidance of a heavenly Father. Miss Taylor went out to China in 1884 in the service of the China Inland Mission, and worked for some time at Tau-chau, a city which lies in the extreme north-west and quite near the Tibetan frontier. In 1887 she paid a visit to the great Lama monastery of Kum-bum, the very monastery in which MM. Huc and Gabet had stayed long before while they were learning the Tibetan language. The memory of these two adventurous priests may have stirred a spirit of imitation in a kindred heart, but what chiefly pressed upon Miss Taylor's thoughts as she stood in the Kum-bum lamasery and looked out to the west, was the vision of that great unevangelized land which stretched beyond the horizon for a thousand miles. That this land was not only shut, but almost hermetically sealed, against foreigners she knew perfectly well. But her dictionary, like Napoleon's, did not contain the word "impossible." She recalled Christ's marching orders to His Church, "Go ye into all the world!" and said to herself, "Our Lord has given us no commands which are impossible to be carried out." And if no one else was ready in Christ's name to try to scale "the roof of the world," and press on into the sacred city of Lhasa itself, she determined that she, at all events, would make the attempt.

Her first idea was to make India her point of departure, for Lhasa lies much nearer to India than to China, though the comparative shortness of this route is balanced by the fact that it leads right over the Himalayas. She went accordingly to Darjeeling, pressed on into Sikkim, which had not yet passed under British rule, and settled down near a Tibetan fort called Kambajong, with the view of mastering the language thoroughly before proceeding any farther. From the first the Tibetan suspicion of all strangers showed itself. The people would often ask her in an unpleasantly suggestive manner what they should do with her body if she died. Her answer was, that she had no intention of dying just then. The intentions of the natives, however, did not coincide with her own, and they next resorted to a custom they have of "praying people dead." Their faith in the power of prayer did not hinder them from giving Heaven some assistance in getting their prayers answered. One day the chief's

PONTSO
Miss Taylor's servant

TAKING TEA IN TIBETAN STYLE

In the centre is Miss Taylor; at the left is Pontso, holding a leather bag of barley flour; on the right is his wife, holding the teapot. The three wooden bowls are the teacups. At the extreme right is a bamboo churn; in front of it goatskin bellows with an iron funnel; and in the centre, in front, are leather bags for tea, butter, etc.

CHURNING TEA

wife invited Miss Taylor to dinner, and set before her an appetizing dish of rice and eggs. She had not long partaken of it when she fell seriously ill, with all the symptoms of aconite poisoning. On her recovery she wisely left this district, and settled down to live the life of the natives themselves in a little hut near the Tibetan monastery of Podang Gumpa.

After a year spent in this way, for ten months of which she never saw the face of a white person, she realized the impracticability of making her way to Lhasa by the Himalayan route, which is far more jealously guarded than the one from the frontiers of China. She decided, therefore, to return to China, and to make it her starting-point. Her time in Sikkim had not been wasted. In the first place, she had not only learned Tibetan thoroughly, but had acquired it in its purest form as spoken at Lhasa. In the next place, she had gained a friend and attendant who was to prove of invaluable service to her in her future wanderings. A young Tibetan named Pontso, a native of Lhasa, had met with a serious accident while travelling on the frontiers of India. Some one directed him to the white lady for treatment. He had never seen a foreigner before, but the kindness and care with which Miss Taylor nursed him in his sufferings completely won his heart. He became a believer in the religion which prompted such goodness to a stranger, devoted himself thenceforth to the service of his benefactress, and justified the trust she placed in him by his unfailing courage and fidelity.

Taking Pontso with her, Miss Taylor now sailed to Shanghai, made her way up the Yang-tse for 2,000 miles, and then on to Tau-chau on the Tibetan frontier. By way of preparing herself still further for her projected march into the interior, she visited a number of lamaseries in that region, made friends with the lamas, and learned everything she could about the Tibetan religion and ways of life and thought.

About a year after her return to Tau-chau the opportunity came for which she had been waiting. Among her acquaintances in the town was a Chinese Mohammedan named

Noga, whose wife, Erminie, was a Lhasa woman. Noga was a trader who had several times been to Lhasa, and on his last journey had brought away this Lhasa wife. According to a Tibetan custom, he had married her only for a fixed term, and as the three years named in the bond were now fully up, Erminie was anxious to return to her native city, and Noga quite willing to convey her back. The only question was one of ways and means, and when they found that Miss Taylor wished to go to Lhasa, Noga made a proposal. He would himself guide her all the way to the capital, provided she supplied the horses and met all necessary expenses. Miss Taylor at once agreed to his terms, which, if the Chinaman had been honest, would have been advantageous to both parties. But Noga was a deep-dyed scoundrel, as Miss Taylor soon discovered to her cost.

It was on the 2nd of September, 1892, that this brave Englishwoman set out on her heroic enterprise. She was accompanied by five Asiatics—Noga and his wife, her faithful attendant Pontso, a young Chinese whom she had engaged as an additional servant, and a Tibetan frontiersman, Nobgey by name, who asked permission to join the little company, as he also was bound for Lhasa. There were sixteen horses in the cavalcade, two mounts being provided for most of the travellers, while there were several pack-horses loaded with tents, bedding, cloth for barter, presents for chiefs, and provisions for two months.

They had not proceeded far into the wild country which begins immediately after the Chinese frontier is left behind, when their troubles commenced. They came suddenly upon a group of eight brigands who were haunting the mountain track for the express purpose of relieving travellers of their valuables. Fortunately the brigands had not noticed their approach, and were seated round a fire enjoying the favourite Tibetan meal of tea—a meal in more senses than one, for Tibetans thicken the beverage with a handful of barley meal, so that it becomes a kind of gruel. Moreover, the robbers were armed with old-fashioned matchlocks, the tinder-boxes of which it took some time to light, and as Miss

Miss Taylor and her Party attacked by Tibetan Brigands

Taylor's party, though weaker in numbers, were better armed, they succeeded in beating off their assailants.

Three days after, they overtook a caravan of friendly Mongols travelling in the same direction as themselves, and in view of their recent experience, thought it wise to amalgamate their forces. Their satisfaction at being thus reinforced was not long-lived. Almost immediately after a band of brigands 200 strong swept down upon the caravan, entirely surrounded it, and began firing from all sides. Two men were killed and seven wounded; resistance was hopeless, and the whole company had to surrender. The Mongols and Nobgey were robbed of everything, and had to turn back; but as the brigand code of honour forbids war upon women, Miss Taylor and her four attendants were allowed to pass on their way, not, however, without being deprived of two of the horses and a good part of the luggage.

The next stage of the journey lay through the land of a strange people known as the Goloks. This is a fierce and warlike race, bearing some resemblance both in habits and dress to the

Scotch Highlanders of other days. They draw up their sheepskin garments by a girdle so as to form a kind of kilt, and leave their knees bare, while covering the lower part of their limbs with cloth leggings fastened with garters of bright-coloured wool. Like the Highlanders of long ago, they have a great contempt for law and authority, and acknowledge neither Tibetan nor Chinese rule. The chief delight of their lives is to engage in forays upon people of more peaceful tastes and habits than themselves. Issuing in large bodies from their mountain glens under some fighting chieftain, they sweep down upon the people of some neighbouring tribe, and carry off as booty their cattle, horses, sheep, tents, and other belongings. Among the Goloks Miss Taylor would have fared even worse than she had already done at the hands of the brigands, but for the fact that the part of the tribe with which she first came in contact was ruled by a chieftainess, a woman named Wachu Bumo. On discovering that this white traveller was also a woman, Wachu Bumo took quite a fancy to her, and not only saw to it that she was treated courteously so long as she remained in the Golok valleys, but insisted on furnishing her with an escort of two Golok horsemen to see her safely on her way for some distance after she had left the country of these marauders.

It is characteristic of Miss Taylor that in her little book, *Pioneering in Tibet*, she says hardly anything about her own hardships and sufferings in that long march through one of the wildest regions of the world. For a great part of the way, it must be remembered, the route ran among mountains covered with perpetual snow. Rivers had to be crossed which knew neither bridge nor ferry nor ford. Winter too was coming on, and they had often to advance in the teeth of blinding storms of sleet and snow. In England Miss Taylor had been considered delicate, but a brave spirit and a strong will carried her through experiences which might well have broken down the strongest physique. Shortly after they had left the land of the Goloks the cold and exposure proved too much for her Chinese servant, a tall, powerful young man. Miss Taylor does not dwell upon the circumstances of his death, but a glimpse like the following is suggestive by its very reticence: "We buried him at noon. A bright sun lightened up the snow-clad hills when the men dug up a few hard sods in some swampy ground close by, laid down the body in its shroud of white cotton cloth, and covered it as best they could with the frost-bound earth. At night the wolves were howling round the grave. This was in the Peigo country."

In a little mountain town called Gala Miss Taylor made the interesting acquaintance of a couple, Pa-tegn and Per-ma, whose marriage had a flavour of romance unusual in Tibet. From infancy Pa-tegn had been dedicated to the priesthood, and had been brought up accordingly in a lamasery. But when about twenty years of age he suddenly fell in love with Per-ma. The course of his true love could not possibly run smooth, for celibacy is as binding on a Buddhist lama as on a Romish priest. But "one fine day," as Miss Taylor puts it, "this Tibetan Abelard disappeared, and in company with Per-ma made his way to Lhasa." Here he discarded his priest's robe and became a tailor. After a child had been born to them they decided to return to Gala, and by means of a judicious present succeeded in soothing the outraged feelings of the local chief. In the house of this couple Miss Taylor stayed for some time to rest from her fatigues, and when she was setting out again persuaded Pa-tegn, who was an experienced traveller and knew Lhasa well, to come with her in place of the Chinese attendant she had recently lost. It was fortunate for her that she secured his services. He proved a capable and devoted follower, and it would have gone ill with her, as she soon found out, but for his presence and help.

They were now in the very heart of the mountains, and Noga, the Chinese guide, feeling that Miss Taylor was thoroughly in his power, began to appear in his true character. Both he and his wife had behaved very badly from the first, but it now became evident that his real purpose all along had been to rob and murder his employer before reaching Lhasa. More than once he made deliberate attempts on her life, but on each occasion the vigilance of

Pontso and Pa-tegn defeated his villainy; and at last he contented himself with deserting her altogether, carrying off at the same time, along with his wife, a horse, a mule, and the larger of the two tents.

The little party of three—Miss Taylor and two Tibetans—was now reduced to such straits for lack of food that the only remaining tent had to be bartered for the necessaries of life; and though it was now the middle of December in that awful climate, they had henceforth to sleep in the open air. When night fell they looked about for holes in the ground, so that they might have a little shelter from the high and piercing winds which in those elevated regions are constantly blowing. A march of several days brought them to the Dam-jau-er-la Pass, one of the loftiest and most dreaded passes in Tibet. Here the cold is so paralysing that it is not uncommon for some travellers in a caravan to be completely overpowered by it, so that they drop down helpless by the wayside. There they are simply left to perish, since any halt on their account might mean death to others of the company.

At length the waters of the Bo-Chu were crossed, the boundary of the sacred province of Ü, in which Lhasa stands, and the goal of the journey seemed almost in sight. But alas for their hopes! In the middle of a deep gorge through which the path ran, two fully armed Tibetan soldiers sprang out from behind the rocks, ordered them to halt, and took them prisoners. This was on January 3rd, 1893. Miss Taylor soon learned to what this arrest was due. Noga, after deserting her, had hurried on in front for the purpose of lodging information that he had met two Tibetans conducting a European lady towards Lhasa. Guards were accordingly placed at all the approaches, and Miss Taylor had walked into a prepared trap. For several days she was kept a prisoner, surrounded by about twenty soldiers, and having no better shelter by day or night than a narrow coffin-shaped hole in the ground. At last she and her two attendants were brought before some chiefs who had been summoned from Lhasa, and a trial was entered into which lasted for days, communication with the capital being kept up all the while by special messengers. Word came from Lhasa that the white lady was to be treated courteously, and this injunction was carefully attended to. But the issue of the trial was never in doubt. When only three days' march from the Sacred City, nearer than any of the later European travellers had succeeded in getting, Miss Taylor had to turn back and retrace every step of the weary way from the frontiers of China.

The return was even more trying than the advance, not only because hope was now turned to disappointment, but because winter in all its rigour now lay upon the land. The Tibetan authorities, though firm, were not unkind, and supplied Miss Taylor with provisions, some money, and two horses. But the Tibetan climate made up for any gentleness on the part of the Lhasa chiefs. The cold was almost unspeakable, and the food they tried to cook over their dung fires had often to be eaten half raw and little more than half warm, since at the great elevations of the mountain passes water boiled with very little heat. For twenty days at a stretch they had to sleep on the ground in the open air, the snow falling around them all the while; for tent they had none, and there was no sign of any human habitation. Their greatest difficulty, however, was to keep their horses from starving in that frozen land. In Tibet the emergency ration for horses in winter is raw goat's flesh, which they eat greedily; but Miss Taylor could not afford to buy goats. All that could be spared to the poor steeds was a little tea with cheese and butter stirred into it, with the result that the famishing animals ate the woollen clothing of their riders whenever they got a chance.

Miss Taylor reached China safely once more, seven months and ten days after she had set out for Lhasa from the city of Tau-chau. She made no further attempt to penetrate to the Sacred City. The very year (1893) which witnessed the discomfiture of her heroic effort was marked by the signing of the Sikkim-Tibet Convention, which secured a trade-mart at Yatung, on the Tibetan side of the Indian frontier, open to all British subjects for the purposes of trade. In this political event Miss Taylor's discerning eye saw a missionary opportunity. From China she returned once more to the Himalayas, and started her remarkable mission at Yatung, in the Chumbi Valley, where by and by she secured the assistance of two other ladies—Miss Ferguson and Miss Foster. Nominally she is a trader, this being the ground of her right to settle down within the borders of the Forbidden Empire, and in point of fact she carries on some trade with the people of the district, who much prefer her dealings to those of the Chinese merchants and officials. But first of all, as both Chinese and Tibetans know, she is a missionary, partly to the bodies (for her mission is provided with a dispensary), but above all to the souls of her beloved Tibetans. "The trading is not a hardship," she writes. "If Paul could make tents for Christ, surely we can do this for our Master. So those who are 'called' to work for Tibet must be prepared for the present to sell goods to the Tibetans or attend to their ailments, as well as preach the Gospel to them." Seldom surely in the annals of Christian missions has there been a more romantic figure than that of this heroine of Tibet, who nearly succeeded in reaching Lhasa, but having failed, turned, with a sanctified common sense which might almost be described as apostolic, to the open door offered by the trading regulations of the Sikkim-Tibet Convention of 1893.

The story of Miss Taylor's march upon Lhasa, together with some account of her pioneer mission in the Chumbi Valley, will be found in her book, *Pioneering in Tibet* (London: Morgan and Scott).

"THE SAVIOUR OF LIAO-YANG"

CHAPTER VI

"THE SAVIOUR OF LIAO-YANG"

A medical missionary's power—The Boxer madness—The avenging Russians—Looting of Hai-cheng—The "Free Healing Hall"—In front of Liao-yang—"A fine thing done by a white man all alone"—"The Saviour of Liao-yang"—Russo-Japanese War—Battle of Liao-yang—A Mission hospital in the hour of battle—Mr. Bennet Burleigh's testimony—A robber's point of view—Adventure with bandits.

IN an earlier chapter on the work of Dr. Chamberlain among the Telugus of south-eastern India, something was said about the romantic aspects of even the ordinary routine of medical missions. Whether in the wards of his hospital or itinerating among scattered villages, the missionary doctor has an opportunity and an influence beyond any possessed by one who is only a preacher or teacher.

Jesus Christ, it has been said, was the first medical missionary. As he went about Galilee doing good, He not only "preached the Gospel of the kingdom," but "healed all manner of sickness and all manner of disease among the people." In this combination of healing with preaching lay a large part of the secret of our Lord's attractive power. The modern missionary doctor cannot work miracles. But through the progress of medical science he has acquired a marvellous power to heal sickness and relieve suffering. And by the quiet exercise of his skill amongst a heathen and sometimes hostile population, he inspires a confidence and calls forth a gratitude by which the solid walls of prejudice are rapidly broken down and locked doors are thrown wide open for the entrance of the Christian Gospel.

It is the gracious work of healing, steadily carried on from year to year, that lays the foundations of a medical missionary's power. But sometimes in the history of a mission there come hours of crisis which bring with them the chance of doing something heroic, and in which a strong man's grandest qualities become revealed. It was in such an hour that Dr. A. Macdonald Westwater, a Scotch Presbyterian missionary, gained the name of "The Saviour of Liao-yang," by which he is now known all over Manchuria.

The Boxer madness had swept up to Manchuria from the south, and had raged across the country with the swift destructiveness of a prairie fire. Hordes of Chinese soldiers joined the anti-foreign movement, and everywhere there was "red ruin and the breaking up of laws." Christian missions and native Christians suffered most, for they had to bear the full brunt of the savage hatred stirred up against the "foreign devils." But the rioters did not stop short with massacring Christians and destroying mission property. Boxerism soon turned to indiscriminate brigandage. And by and by the great city of Mukden, the capital of the three provinces of Manchuria, was looted, while for a distance of 500 miles the marauders marched along the railway line, tearing up the rails, destroying stations, plundering and burning houses and villas on either hand.

But the avengers were soon on the trail. Russian troops were poured into Manchuria, and a terrible work of reprisal was begun. Advancing simultaneously from south and north, the Russians simply wiped out every village in which they found any railway material, and left the country behind them black and smoking on both sides of what had once been the railway line.

The terror of their name travelled before them. As they drew near to Hai-cheng the people fled *en masse*, though the better-off among them, in the hope of securing some consideration for their property, took the precaution of leaving caretakers behind in their houses and shops. But the troops of the Czar treated Hai-cheng as they had already treated many a meaner place. Of the numerous caretakers left in the city only six escaped from the pitiless massacre that followed the military occupation. Hai-cheng itself was looted and left absolutely bare. And then the Russians moved onwards, still destroying as they went, and making their way now towards the important city of Liao-yang.

In Liao-yang, previous to the Boxer outbreak, a splendid work had been carried on for years by Dr. Westwater, an agent of the United Presbyterian, now the United Free

Church of Scotland. His "Free Healing Hall," as the name of his mission hospital ran in Chinese, had become a place of note in the city. In this hall, as one of the citizens, not himself a Christian, expressed it, "the blind saw, the lame walked, the deaf heard; and all were counselled to virtue."

Compelled by the Boxer fury to lay down his work in Liao-yang for a time, the doctor sought and obtained permission to accompany the Russian punitive field force as a member of the Russian Red Cross Society with General Alexandrovski at its head. He was present in every battle fought during the campaign, and immensely impressed the Russian officers by his surgical skill, which quite surpassed that of any doctor of their own. In this way he gained the good opinion and respect of the general in command, and was able to do something towards checking the frightful excesses of which, at first, the army was guilty.

When the advancing troops reached Liao-yang, a small engagement was fought in which the Chinese were defeated. Following up their victory, the Russians were just about to enter the suburbs, when they were fired upon from the city walls and so brought to a halt. Meanwhile from the Korean Gate the inhabitants were pouring out in crowds, endeavouring to make good their escape before the Russians should take the city. Numbers of people were trampled to death in the panic-stricken rush, many were pushed into the river and drowned. To crown the horrors of the scene, the Russian gunners got on to this black mass of struggling fugitives, and began to throw shells into the thick of it.

It now seemed certain that Liao-yang would share the fate that had already befallen Hai-cheng—the fate of being deserted by a terrified population and given up to massacre and loot at the hands of native brigands as well as of Russian troops. Only one man stood between it and destruction, but that man had the soul of a hero, and proved himself equal to the occasion.

Before the general had ordered an assault upon the city, Dr. Westwater had obtained an interview with him. His words were brief but to the point. "I undertake," he said, "to enter Liao-yang by myself, and to persuade the people to surrender peacefully, but upon one condition." "What is that?" asked the general. "That I have your solemn word of honour that no harm shall be done to the person of man or woman within the walls, and that there shall be absolutely no looting."

To a Russian commander this was a new way of dealing with an obstinate Chinese town. But Dr. Westwater's personality by this time had made a strong impression on him, and he at once gave his word of honour to observe the stipulated terms. The doctor then mounted his pony, and rode on all alone towards the walls of this lately Boxerised city.

Obtaining entrance by one of the gates, and riding on through the streets, he could see no sign of any living creature. It looked at first as if the whole population had already vanished, though most of them, he afterwards found, had simply shut themselves up within their houses. At last a Christian schoolboy approached who had recognized him and come out to meet him. From this boy Dr. Westwater learned that at that very time the members of the

Guild—the City Fathers of Liao-yang, as they might be called—were gathered together to take counsel regarding the city's fate.

Riding on, he came to their hall of meeting, and introduced himself as one whom most of them knew as a Christian doctor, but who was now come as an ambassador of peace from the head of the Russian army. And when he went on to inform them that the general had passed his deliberate word of honour to himself to do no harm to the place if it was quietly surrendered, a thrill of astonishment and relief ran through the meeting. The word was quickly carried through the streets, and the confidence of the city was restored as if by magic. The people no longer thought of abandoning Liao-yang to its fate, but prepared with perfect calmness to receive their conquerors.

The Russian general, on the other hand, was absolutely loyal to his word. To secure that his promises should be observed to the letter he appointed, not sergeants merely, but commissioned officers to go about the streets with the patrols. And this was the altogether unexampled result. During the whole of the

Russian occupation of Liao-yang there was not a single instance of crime committed by the soldiery against the person or property of any inhabitant of the city.

This gallant deed of the Scotch missionary doctor has been described by Mr. Whigham, the well-known Eastern traveller and war correspondent, as "a fine thing done by a white man all alone," and as the bravest deed of which he knows.[1] And it was this that gained for Dr. Westwater from the people of Manchuria his enviable name of "The Saviour of Liao-yang."

Upon the citizens of Liao-yang itself Dr. Westwater's action made a very deep impression. They felt that to him they owed the salvation of their lives and homes. On his return to the city after the conclusion of his period of service with the Red Cross Society, the heads of the native guilds called on him to express their gratitude. They offered him the choice of a number of compounds for a temporary house and hospital, stating their readiness to pay all the expenses of alterations,

[1] See *The Bravest Deed I Ever Saw* (Hutchinson and Co.), p. 37.

rent, and even of medicines. Finally, about a year after, when he went home to Scotland on furlough, the city honoured him with a triumphal procession. Banners waved, musical instruments brayed and banged. With native dignity and grandeur the gentry of the place accompanied the man whom they delighted to honour through the streets, out of the gate, and right up to the railway station, where they bade him their best farewell.

As the result of what he had done, the doctor's name and fame spread far and wide through the provinces of Manchuria. Some time afterwards the Rev. Mr. MacNaughtan, going on a prolonged and distant missionary tour, found that right away to the banks of the Yalu River, some 200 miles from Liao-yang, Dr. Westwater's was a name to charm with. Immediately on hearing it mentioned the people would say, "Oh, that was the man who saved Liao-yang."

Hardly less deep was the effect produced by the doctor's character and action upon the Russians in Manchuria. His opinions had weight with the authorities, while he himself became a great personal favourite with all who knew him. Being a Scotchman, Muscovite demonstrativeness often caused him some embarrassment, for a Russian admirer thought nothing of throwing his arms round him and bestowing a hearty kiss. Mr. Whigham tells how he met a Russian engineer, M. Restzoff, who, learning that Mr. Whigham was a Scotchman, said he was glad to make the acquaintance of one who came from Scotland, for the two greatest men he knew of were both Scotchmen—Dr. Westwater and Sir Walter Scott!

Much water has flowed under the bridges of Manchuria—water often mingled with blood—since the days of the Boxer rising. But the events of more recent years have only added to Dr. Westwater's reputation, and proved once more how much can be done in the interests of humanity and Christianity, amid all "the tumult and the shouting" and the unbridled savagery of war, by a brave, strong man who has devoted his life to the service of his fellow-creatures as a medical missionary.

When the tremendous struggle began between Japan and Russia, Dr. Westwater and his colleague, Mr. MacNaughtan, together with their wives, were allowed to remain in Liao-yang. This in itself was a tribute to the Doctor's influence, for it is practically certain that but for him the Russians would have expelled the missionaries from the province with the opening of the war. It was the entire confidence felt in him—sufficiently proved by his being in constant demand at headquarters to prescribe for the officers of the army—that enabled the mission to retain its hold upon the city right through the long period of stress and conflict.

As General Kuropatkin had fixed his headquarters at Liao-yang, every fresh disaster to the Russian forces sent an electric thrill through the whole region of which the city formed the centre. And as the opposing armies drew nearer and nearer, the Russians constantly retreating and the Japanese pressing on, the surrounding population began to flock into Liao-yang by tens of thousands. At this stage the doctor obtained General Kuropatkin's permission to open a refuge for these poor homeless creatures, and soon he had four thousand of them, all heathen, under his immediate care.

Meanwhile the tide of battle rolled nearer and nearer. From Mr. MacNaughtan's lips we have received a vivid account of the scenes which were witnessed by Dr. Westwater and himself from the city walls during that long-drawn week of desperate and Titanic encounter which is known as the battle of Liao-yang. Everything lay before them as in a vast panorama—the great Manchurian plain rolling out its length towards the boundary of the distant low hills, the constant stream of ammunition and commissariat waggons flowing on steadily from the station to the battlefield, the sad stream of wounded men flowing as steadily back, the deadly shells bursting nearer and nearer until at length it became no longer possible to stand in safety on the city walls.

Then, after the days of waiting and watching, followed the days of strenuous action. Men, women, and little children, horribly smashed up, began to be carried into the mission hospital, till not only the wards but all the surrounding sheds were crammed with patients.

Meanwhile the doctor had his crowded refuge to think of and provide for and be anxious about, for the shells were falling thick, and five times it was hit, though by a merciful providence on every occasion not a single soul within the walls was so much as scratched.

In his *Empire of the East* Mr. Bennet Burleigh, the veteran *doyen* of military correspondents, describes Dr. Westwater as he found him in the thick of his work at this decisive moment of the war. "Brave as a lion," he writes, "Dr. Westwater went about alone, regardless of shellfire and bullets, succouring the wounded and doing good." And then he goes on to tell in more detail what kind of good the doctor was doing in those awful days: how he sheltered the homeless, fed the starving, performed under all the strain of multiplied duties scores of critical operations, and yet found time to show pity and kindness to the crowds of terrified women and helpless children whom war had cast upon his hands.

"I saw the doctor," he says, "just after he had completed seven amputations, and a score more of cases remained to be dealt with." It adds to the impressiveness of Mr. Bennet Burleigh's picture of a hero at the post of duty in a trying hour when he remarks: "He had no assistant—his only helpers a few Chinese who served as nurses." We should supplement Mr. Burleigh's statement, however, by mentioning that while Dr. Westwater was ministering to the heathen refugees, Mr. MacNaughtan, by previous arrangement with his colleague, was devoting himself to the service of the native Christians of Liao-yang in the hour of need.

When the Japanese at length entered the city, they paid their tribute, like the Russians before them, to the value of Dr. Westwater's work. It was their fire, of course, that had wrought the havoc among the non-combatants, but this was an inevitable result of the fact that the Russians had made their last stand at the railway station, and no one more regretted the suffering caused to the people of Liao-yang than the victorious general. One of his first acts was to contribute 1000 yen to Dr. Westwater's hospital and the same sum to his refuge, i.e. in English money, £100 to each.

We have shown something of Dr. Westwater's renown among Chinese citizens and English war correspondents, among the warriors of Russia and Japan alike. It is half amusing to learn that he holds a reputation hardly less distinguished among the robbers and bandits of the Manchurian wilds.

These outlaws, the pests of the country in troublous times, have a happy facility of becoming armed marauders or peaceful villagers at will. The advantages of the doctor's "Free Healing Hall" to a man with a broken limb or an unextracted bullet are not unknown to them, and now and then a robber wounded in some skirmish will find his way into the hospital at Liao-yang, representing himself as a poor peasant who has been attacked and wounded by cruel bandits.

Some time ago a Christian colporteur from the city was travelling through the country districts with his pack of Bibles, Testaments, and tracts. He was passing along a road bordered by a field of ripe millet, when in a moment three or four robbers armed with revolvers sprang out from their hiding-place behind the tall stalks. First of all they relieved him of the money made by his sales, then they opened his pack and looked curiously at his books. "Who are you?" one of them asked. "I belong to the Bible Society," he said. "What is that?" "It is a society of Christians," the man replied. "Ah! Christians!" they shouted, "the society of the foreign devils"; and with that one of them pointed his revolver at the colporteur's head, fingering the trigger meanwhile in a way that was decidedly nasty.

Just then another of the band suddenly stepped foward and asked, "Do you know Dr. Westwater?" "I know him well," the man answered; "he is a member of the Church to which I belong." On hearing this the robber turned to his companions and said, "Do not touch this fellow. Dr. Westwater is a good man. Two years ago he took a bullet out of my ribs." Whereupon this robber band handed back to the colporteur not only his pack, but every copper of his money, and bade him go in peace on his way to Liao-yang.

Another experience of a somewhat similar

kind befell the doctor's colleague, the Rev. Mr. MacNaughtan himself. About a fortnight before the outbreak of the Russo-Japanese War, Mr. MacNaughtan, who had been itinerating in the province, was riding back to Liao-yang. He was drawing near to a strange village, and there was nothing on the road in front of him but a Chinese cart rumbling slowly along. All at once there shot out from the village in a fan-shaped skirmishing formation a band of about twenty horsemen, all armed with rifles. Some of them galloped furiously to right and left, so as to cut off any possibility of escape, but five came straight down the road towards the carter and the missionary.

They met the carter first. One of them, who was mounted on a tall Russian horse, taken no doubt from a murdered Russian soldier, drew up his steed across the road, compelling the cart to stop, and then drawing a heavy whip, began to lash the unfortunate peasant from head to heel.

Mr. MacNaughtan's heart beat fast, for he knew that at that very time Russian outposts were being nipped off every now and then by bands of desperate bandits. He did not know what might be about to befall him. But he thought it best, trusting in God, to put a brave face on the matter and ride straight on.

When he reached the cart the five robbers were drawn up beside it on the road. One of them held his rifle across his saddle ready for use, and all of them looked at him keenly. That he was a European they saw at once, but the Chinese sheepskin robe he wore showed that he was not a Russian, but a missionary. "Where are you going?" they demanded. "To Liao-yang," he replied. "Then pass on," they said. And without the slightest attempt on the part of any one of them to deprive him of his money or to molest him in any way, he was allowed to continue on his journey.

Talking to the present writer of this incident, Mr. MacNaughtan said that he had no doubt whatever that, though not himself a doctor, he owed his escape to the influence of the Liao-yang medical mission. Even to the savage bandits of Manchuria Dr. Westwater is "a good man." Some of them, as has been said, have passed through his hands, and are grateful to him accordingly. Others have heard of his skill and generosity, and if on no higher grounds, entertain a kindly feeling towards him at least from the lower but still effective motive of that form of gratitude which has been defined as "a lively sense of favours to come."

The materials for the above chapter have been derived partly from the pages of the *Missionary Record* of the United Free Church of Scotland, but chiefly from the personal narrative of the Rev. W. MacNaughtan, M.A., of the Presbyterian Mission in Liao-yang.